Slave Rebellions

Other titles in this series:

Slave Rebellions

Lucent Library of Black History

Jessica A. Gresko

LUCENT BOOKS

An imprint of Thomson Gale, a part of The Thomson Corporation

Detroit • New York • San Francisco • San Diego • New Haven, Conn.
Waterville, Maine • London • Munich

LIBRARY OF CONGRESS CATALOGING-IN-PUBLICATION DATA

Gresko, Jessica A.
Slave rebellions / Jessica A. Gresko.
    p. cm. — (Lucent library of black history)
Includes bibliographical references and index.
Audience: Grade 5–8.
ISBN 1-59018-548-X (hardcover : alk. paper)
1. Slave insurrections—United States—HIstory—Juvenile literature. 2. Slavery—United States—History—Juvenile literature. 3. African Americans—History—Juvenile literature. I. Title.
E447.G74 2007
306.3'620973—dc22

2006018812

Printed in the United States of America

Contents

Foreword

It has been more than five hundred years since Africans were first brought to the New World in shackles, and over 140 years since slavery was formally abolished in the United States. Over 50 years have passed since the fallacy of "separate but equal" was obliterated in the American courts, and some forty years since the watershed Civil Rights Act of 1965 guaranteed the rights and liberties of all Americans, especially those of color. Over time, these changes have become celebrated landmarks in American history. In the twenty-first century, African American men and women are politicians, judges, diplomats, professors, deans, doctors, artists, athletes, business owners, and home owners. For many, the scars of the past have melted away in the opportunities that have been found in contemporary society. Observers such as Peter N. Kirsanow, who sits on the U.S. Commission of Civil Rights, point to these accomplishments and conclude, "The growing black middle class may be viewed as proof that most of the civil rights battles have been won."

In spite of these legal victories, however, prejudice and inequality have persisted in American society. In 2003, African Americans comprised just 12 percent of the nation's population, yet accounted for 44 percent of its prison inmates and 24 percent of its poor. Racially motivated hate crimes continue to appear on the pages of major newspapers in many American cities. Furthermore, many African Americans still experience either overt or muted racism in their daily lives. A 1996 study undertaken by Professor Nancy Krieger of the Harvard School of Public Health, for example, found that 80 percent of the African American participants reported having experienced racial discrimination in one or more settings, including at work or school, applying for housing and medical care, from the police or in the courts, and on the street or in a public setting.

It is for these reasons that many believe the struggle for racial equality and justice is far from over. These episodes of discrimination threaten to shatter the illusion that America has completely overcome its racist past, causing many black Americans to become increasingly frustrated and confused. Scholar and writer Ellis Cose has described this splintered state in the following way: "I have done everything I was supposed to do. I have stayed out of trouble with the law, gone to the right schools, and worked myself nearly to death. What more do they want? Why in God's name won't they accept me as a full human being?" For Cose and others, the struggle for equality and justice has yet to be fully achieved.

In many subtle yet important ways the traumatic experiences of slavery and segregation continue to inform the way race is discussed and experienced in the twenty-first century. Indeed, it is possible that America will always grapple with the fallout from its distressing past. Ulric Haynes, dean of the Hofstra University School of Business has said, "Perhaps race will always matter, given the historical circumstances under which we came to this country." But studying this past and understanding how it contributes to present-day dialogues about race and history in America is a critical component of contemporary education. To this end, the Lucent Library of Black History offers a thorough look at the experiences that have shaped the black community and the American people as a whole. Annotated bibliographies provide readers with ideas for further research, while fully documented primary and secondary source quotations enhance the text. Each book in the series explores a different episode of black history; together they provide students with a wealth of information as well as launching points for further study and discussion.

Slaveholders' Worst Nightmare

Fear had kept one Virginia resident and his wife awake at night for three months when the man wrote to a friend in 1831. He confessed that he and his wife were terrified to go to bed. "Our nights are sometimes spent in listening to noises," he wrote.

The man's alarm was understandable. That year, a slave named Nat Turner had led a bold slave rebellion near the man's home. Beginning with a nighttime attack, the brazen rebels killed more than fifty people before being stopped by the militia, and the act had shocked white citizens. The letter writer said he was not the only one who was shaken. "There has been and there still is a *panic* in all this country," he wrote.[1]

In fact, fear that those they held as property might rise in rebellion was widespread among white slaveholders from colonial times to the outbreak of the Civil War in 1861. From the first time slaves were brought to the United States until slavery was abolished after the Civil War, rebellion was an ever-present threat. Especially in the South, where slavery was an integral part of life and where most of the slaves in the country were held, fears of rebellion ran high. Though authorities created strict laws and harsh punishments for slaves who gathered together, these attempts to prevent slaves from plotting uprisings were never completely effective. Slaves still found ways to plan and carry out rebellions.

Indeed, slave rebellions were fairly common. According to one historian's count, there were over 250 documented slave uprisings in America in which ten or more slaves participated. The number of rebellions swells to several hundred when smaller plots, those involving three or more slaves, are counted. Severe punishment and even the threat of death could not stop slaves determined to strike out at their oppressors, and the names of rebel leaders like Gabriel Prosser, Denmark Vesey, Nat Turner, and Cinqué became the stuff of legend.

Individual rebellions differed from each other in striking ways. For example, some rebels targeted whites living in large communities while others planned rampages through the countryside. Some rebels plotted for years, waiting for the right moment, while others acted more spontaneously.

The outcomes of slave rebellions varied as well. Some uprisings achieved their leaders' goals of causing death and destruction. Others failed utterly or were discovered before they began. Whatever their outcome, slave rebellions all thoroughly unnerved white people throughout the states where slavery was allowed. Night after night, slave owners and their families went to bed with at least some sense that they were at risk—that somewhere in the slave quarters someone might be awaiting the opportunity to rise up and strike a deadly blow for freedom.

Chapter One

Slavery and Slave Rebellions in America

Slave rebellions were a powerful and frightening reality in America from 1619, when the first slaves were brought to the British colonies, up to the close of the Civil War in 1865, when slavery in America was finally outlawed. These rebellions often came as a shock to slave owners and other white citizens, but slaves never stopped longing for a way out of the harsh and often brutal conditions imposed on them. It is not surprising that many looked for any opportunity to rebel.

Slavery Comes to America

The story of American slavery begins during colonial times. Colonists came from England to settle the newly discovered North American lands in the late sixteenth century. They built homes and carved farms from the wilderness. But the colonists found they needed more laborers to tend to their crops. At first, much of this work was done by indentured servants. Most indentured servants were poor men and women who came from England. They promised to work for a specified period of time, usually several years, in exchange for payment of their transatlantic passage. Once they finished with their indenture, they were free to start new lives in the colonies.

After a while, the flow of indentured servants slowed. Economic conditions in England improved, and fewer people needed or were willing to become indentured servants. At this point colonists began to look to Africa for laborers. Africa, after all, already had an established slave trade, and Europeans tapped into this market.

Eventually, a system called the triangle trade developed. Slave traders would sail from Europe to Africa with a cargo of

Traders examine a slave upon his arrival in Jamestown, Virginia, in the 1600s.

textiles, rum, and firearms. They traded these goods for slaves. The slaves would then be taken to the New World—usually the Caribbean—where they were sold or traded for goods like sugar, tobacco, and cotton. Then traders sailed back to Europe, sold these goods, and purchased items for trading in Africa, and the cycle began again. The trade was enormous; and historians estimate that between 12 and 20 million Africans were taken from their homes and brought to the New World in this way.

Taken

The African men and women who were sent in chains to the New World became enslaved in numerous ways. Tribal warfare provided one avenue for traders to obtain slaves. Victorious tribes sold prisoners captured during wars in exchange for fabric, rum, and other goods. Slave traders encouraged these wars because they brought more captives. Another way traders obtained slaves was through raids carried out by both African and European men. During a raid, the men would burn a whole village and capture the fleeing villagers. Some Africans were sold into slavery as punishment for a crime. Other slaves were kidnapped—either while they were working in the fields or simply walking alone near their village.

Cinqué, a slave who headed the rebellion aboard the ship *Amistad* in 1839, explained that he had been taken this way. A rice farmer with a wife and three children, Cinqué had owed money to an acquaintance. When Cinqué was unable to repay the loan, the man had him kidnapped and sold to a slave trader; the money the man received for Cinqué settled the debt.

Once taken from their villages, slaves were sold to a trader. These unscrupulous merchants maintained forts along Africa's coast where the slaves were housed before they were resold to other slave traders from many countries, including America, Spain, and Portugal. These slave traders inspected the slaves and chose the individuals who looked strongest and healthiest. To judge their fitness, traders poked and prodded slaves. Sometimes the traders had the slaves open their mouths to inspect their teeth or had them jump up and down. Then the buyer and seller haggled over prices.

Slaves plead with their captors for a chance to breathe fresh air above deck on their crowded ship.

The Middle Passage and Sale

Being captured and sold was only the beginning of a slave's ordeal. Once sold, slaves were loaded onto ships for the journey to the New World. During the two months or more it took to cross the Atlantic Ocean, slaves endured horrific conditions. For most of the journey, several hundred slaves were packed together and chained in the ship's dark, hot hold with little or no room to move and little fresh air. The hold reeked of human waste. If they were lucky, sometimes the ship's captain allowed the slaves to exercise on the ship's deck.

Disease spread rapidly under these conditions, and many captives died on the journey. Severe diarrhea and scurvy were common causes of death, as were outbreaks of smallpox and measles. Slaves who died were simply thrown overboard.

Some slaves were desperate to get out of the miserable conditions aboard the slave ships. They tried to commit suicide,

Olaudah Equiano

One of the most widely read and often-quoted narratives describing the Middle Passage was written by Olaudah Equiano, a former slave. In his 1789 autobiography, Equiano tells readers that he was born in a village in what is now Nigeria. At the age of eleven, he was kidnapped and taken to the New World. He describes the slave ship and the voyage this way:

> I was soon put down under the decks, and there I received such a salutation in my nostrils as I had never experienced in my life: so that, with the loathsomeness of the stench, and crying together, I became so sick and low that I was not able to eat, nor had I the least desire to taste any thing. I now wished for the last friend, death, to relieve me; but soon, to my grief, two of the white men offered me eatables; and, on my refusing to eat, one of them held me fast by the hands, and laid me across I think the windlass, and tied my feet, while the other flogged me severely. I had never experienced any thing of this kind before . . . could I have got over the nettings, I would have jumped over the side, but I could not; and, besides, the crew used to watch us very closely who were not chained down to the decks, lest we should leap into the water: and I have seen some of these poor African prisoners most severely cut for attempting to do so, and hourly whipped for not eating.

Equiano was eventually able to buy his freedom and became a seaman, traveling the world. Later, he settled in London, where he wrote his autobiography. The book quickly became a best seller and made Equiano a wealthy man.

Recently, scholars have questioned passages in Equiano's account. One historian believes that Equiano may have been born in South Carolina and that he combined the stories of other slaves into his autobiography, but the evidence is inconclusive. Equiano's story remains an important source of information about the slave trade and life as a slave.

Olaudah Equiano, *The Interesting Narrative of the Life of Olaudah Equiano, or Gustavus Vassa.* London, 1789. Available online at Project Gutenberg, www.gutenberg.org/etext/15399.

jumping overboard while on deck. Others refused to eat or were too sick to do so. Knowing that a dead slave was a lost investment, slave traders whipped those who refused to eat or force-fed them.

Once across the Atlantic Ocean, slave ships docked at a number of ports in North America or the Caribbean. Their human cargo was then sold at slave markets or auctions. One traveler described an auction he witnessed in Richmond, Virginia, in 1861 this way:

> At length a little bustle occurred at the back of the room, and a fine-looking coloured man was [brought forward]. He walked straight up to the block, mounted it, and put himself in a most dignified attitude. . . . Some of the buyers stopped him during his walk and asked him a variety of questions, as to last employment, state of his health, and so forth. Then they turned his head to the light, and lifted the corners of his eyes, to ascertain whether they were free from indications of disease; in the same way they examined his teeth.[2]

Slaves from Africa and those born in the colonies to slave parents were sold in the same manner. Children born to slaves in the colonies also became slaves, and masters could sell their slave property at any time. Slave families feared being split apart in this cruel fashion.

Life as a Slave

Whether they came from Africa or were born in the New World, slaves were destined to spend their lives working for an owner who dictated how they used almost every waking moment. Farmers owned most of the slaves in the colonies. Slaves worked on cotton, indigo, rice, sugarcane, and tobacco farms. Some of these plantations were large and had over one hundred slaves. Most plantations were smaller, with twenty or fewer slaves. Some slaves worked as domestic servants, cooking and cleaning for their masters or taking care of their children. More slaves did backbreaking work in the field planting and then bringing in the crops.

Regardless of where they worked, slaves had exhausting jobs. Many also lived in daily fear of their masters' wrath. Slaves could be severely punished for even the smallest missteps. Overfilling a teacup could be cause for a whipping.

In this 1860s photo, a slave stands with his hands tied to a whipping post as his master prepares to beat him.

Years after she was freed, Sarah Ross described the way she and other slaves were punished at the plantation where she lived in Benton County, Mississippi: "Frequently the thighs of the male slaves were gashed with a saw and salt put in the wound as a means of punishment for some misdemeanor," she remembered. "The female slaves often had their hair cut off, especially those who had long beautiful hair."[3]

On large plantations, overseers in the fields monitored slaves while they worked. Like the plantation owner, these men were entitled to punish slaves who displeased them. They were as tough or tougher than the owners, whipping slaves if they did not work fast enough or hard enough.

Finally, the slaves' day was not finished when they were through with their master's work. Slaves often returned to their quarters and worked a small plot of their own land and cooked and cleaned for their own families.

Forms of Rebellion

Under such harsh conditions, it is not surprising that many slaves harbored deep anger toward their masters and dreamed of escape. But harsh punishments awaited runaways who were caught and slaves who dared to openly defy their masters. As a result, slaves rebelled in many ways, some subtle, others much less so. Historian Herbert Aptheker has explained: "Sabotage, shamming illness, 'stealing,' suicide and self-mutilation, and strikes were other devices which plagued slave-holders. The carelessness and deliberate destructiveness of the slaves, resulting in broken fences, spoiled tools, and neglected animals, were common."[4] These acts of rebellion undoubtedly angered slave owners. They were both angered and frightened by reports of arson, poisoning, and murder. Many of these rebellious acts, however, involved only one slave whose anger toward a master boiled over in violence. Organized, wide-scale rebellion planned and carried out by slaves generated a whole new category of fear. Whites were terrified of this form of rebellion.

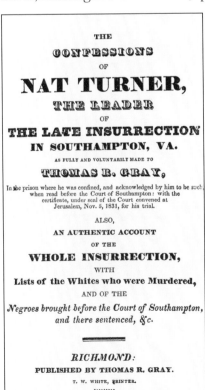

THE

CONFESSIONS

OF

NAT TURNER,

THE LEADER

OF

THE LATE INSURRECTION

IN SOUTHAMPTON, VA.

AS FULLY AND VOLUNTARILY MADE TO

THOMAS R. GRAY,

In the prison where he was confined, and acknowledged by him to be such when read before the Court of Southampton: with the certificate, under seal of the Court convened at Jerusalem, Nov. 5, 1831, for his trial.

ALSO,

AN AUTHENTIC ACCOUNT

OF THE

WHOLE INSURRECTION,

WITH

Lists of the Whites who were Murdered,

AND OF THE

Negroes brought before the Court of Southampton, and there sentenced, &c.

RICHMOND:

PUBLISHED BY THOMAS R. GRAY.

T. W. WHITE, PRINTER.

1832.

The title page from an 1832 book entices readers by offering an "authentic account" of the slave rebellion led by Nat Turner.

Mass Uprisings

The earliest recorded slave rebellion in America dates to 1663. The uprising took place in Gloucester County, in the colony of Virginia, and involved both indentured white servants and black slaves. The plot, however, was discovered before it could be carried out, and those who had planned it paid with their lives. The bloody heads of several of the conspirators were hung from area chimneys to warn any others who might harbor thoughts of rebellion. The man who had betrayed the plot

Rebellion Whispered in the Slave Quarters

■

Though masters tried to keep the news of uprisings from their slaves, word did travel, according to one ex-slave, Daniel Goddard. Goddard was born in South Carolina in 1863, just before the end of the Civil War. Later, he recalled that his parents often talked about rebellions. He was able to relate details of the uprising aboard the ship *Amistad* as well as earlier rebellions, though all happened before he was born. His parents clearly felt these were important pieces of history for him to know. Interviewed as part of a history project sponsored by the government in the 1930s, Goddard remembered:

> Now you ask, if I heard about escapes of slaves. Sure I did and I
> heard my parents discuss the effort of slaves to shake off the
> shackles. . . . The Nat Turner insurrection in Virginia and the
> Vesey uprising in Charleston was discussed often, in my presence,
> by my parents and friends. I learned that revolts of slaves in Mar-
> tinique, Antigua, Santiago, Caracas and [Tortugas], was known all
> over the South. Slaves were about as well aware of what was going
> on as their masters were. However the masters made it harder for
> their slaves for a while.

Stiles M. Scruggs, "Daniel Goddard," in *Born in Slavery: Slave Narratives from the Federal Writers' Project, 19, 1936–1938*. Washington, DC: Library of Congress, Manuscript Division.

was granted his freedom and 5,000 pounds (2,270kg) of tobacco as a reward.

For the next two hundred years, rebellions were a constant reality for slaveholders. Like the Gloucester County rebellion, some uprisings were planned by whites who disagreed with slavery or who sympathized with slaves. Most, however, involved only slaves or, occasionally, free blacks who sought to aid those who were enslaved.

Rebellion Records

Historical accounts of slave rebellions are often unreliable. Records of trials and investigations have disappeared over the years. Sometimes few records of an uprising were kept at all. Accounts were often printed in contemporary newspapers, but many of these were wildly inaccurate. In many cases, local officials made a point of suppressing the facts after a plot was discovered or after a rebellion actually took place. They reasoned that if other slaves learned what had happened they might be encouraged to stage similar uprisings. For all these reasons, details of an uprising could be hard to come by. In 1800, Vice President Thomas Jefferson expressed his frustration in getting news about Gabriel's rebellion plot. Writing to his friend James Monroe, the governor of Virginia, where the rebellion plot had been uncovered, Jefferson said he was sorry he had not seen Monroe. "I wished to learn something of the excitements, the expectations & extent of this negro conspiracy, not being satisfied with the popular reports,"[5] he wrote.

Even when the facts about an uprising or plot were known, written accounts of the incident were still often wrong. Residents and newspaper editors heard rumors and repeated them as truth in letters and newspaper articles. The problem was compounded in locations far away from a rebellion site. Far-flung newspapers that wanted to print news of an uprising relied on reports from travelers or correspondents whose information was not always reliable. Sometimes these reporters made assumptions that they passed along as facts. Many of them received their information second hand, meaning that news was delayed and often distorted.

This was the case after Nat Turner's rebellion in 1831. Rumors that Nat Turner was dead and that the rebels numbered more than one thousand proved untrue. Thomas R. Gray, a lawyer who wrote the fullest account of the rebellion, had heard so much misinformation being repeated as fact that he began his report by saying, "The late insurrection in Southampton has greatly excited the public mind, and led to a thousand idle, exaggerated and mischievous reports."[6] Sorting fact from fiction was one of the reasons he was writing, he said.

Sunday Uprisings

Despite the exaggerations and sketchiness in the accounts of slave rebellions, historians have enough information to note some similarities between uprisings. For example, slaves planning large-scale rebellions often chose the weekend to carry out their plot. On weekends, slaves were allowed a small amount of free time. It was therefore easier for conspirators to leave the plantation without raising suspicions.

Second, many of the men who planned rebellions had advantages and freedoms rarely granted to slaves. For example, some rebel leaders could read, a skill that slaves were usually prohibited from learning. Reading gave them additional access to information and likely a status above their peers. Many of the men who became rebel leaders were permitted to move about freely. Often, their masters had allowed them to hire out, working for others. One rebel leader, Denmark Vesey, was actually a free black man.

Once a rebellion began, it usually proceeded slowly. The rebels were usually on foot, traveling through countryside that featured few roads but many rivers that were bridged in only a few places. Under such circumstances, it would be many hours before other plantations were alerted that anything out of the ordinary was under way.

Finally, one common feature of almost all major slave rebellions is what happened in the aftermath of the rebellion or after the plot was discovered. Almost without fail, the fear that the uprisings generated resulted in a wave of legislation that imposed new restrictions on blacks or mandated increased white policing of the slave population. For example, after the Stono uprising in 1739, South Carolina slaves were prohibited from carrying weapons and from traveling in groups larger than seven without

John Brown's Raid

John Brown's raid on Harper's Ferry is one famous example where blacks and whites joined together to oppose slavery by violent means. On October 17, 1859, a group of twenty-one men led by white abolitionist John Brown attacked a federal arsenal in Virginia. In the group were five black men. Brown's plan was to take some 100,000 muskets and rifles stored in the arsenal and distribute them to local slaves. Once the slaves were armed, he planned to lead them on an invasion of the South.

Brown and his followers did not get far. The men stormed the arsenal and took several white hostages. But local farmers, store owners, and militiamen soon learned of the raid. The next day, federal troops arrived. Using sledgehammers and a makeshift battering ram, the troops forced their way inside the building. Ten of Brown's men were killed, and Brown was later hanged.

Though Brown's raid was unsuccessful, historians generally agree that the rebellion pushed the country in the direction of civil war. Southern slave owners, fearful that other abolitionists would lead slave rebellions, took measures to defend their property.

John Brown, gun raised overhead, defends himself while leading an arsenal raid in Virginia in 1859.

a white escort. A similar tightening of restrictions happened in 1822, after Denmark Vesey's uprising in Charleston. A new group of 150 guards was established to patrol the city around the clock, and authorities imposed new taxes on free blacks like Vesey, hoping to drive them out of the city altogether.

An End to Slavery

By the 1840s, slavery in the United States had become an all-consuming issue, and North and South were increasingly divided over a variety of issues. Northern states had enacted gradual emancipation laws, and both black and white abolitionists were calling for an end to slavery. The system was no longer sustainable or morally correct, they said. Despite the best efforts of the abolitionists and others opposed to slavery, Southern states resisted any change. Slave owners' reactions to rebellion, meanwhile, showed just how determined they were to hold on to their way of life.

Eventually, the issues tearing at the nation became too much. When Abraham Lincoln was elected president in 1860, South Carolina seceded from the union. Other Southern states soon followed and formed the Confederate States of America. President Lincoln refused to accept the South's secession, vowing to use force to preserve the Union if necessary. On April 12, 1861, North and South went to war. Over the next four years, the North and South engaged in the bloodiest conflict in American history. More than 600,000 Americans died in the war that ravaged the country.

Ultimately, the South surrendered. Though the war was not solely about slavery, the bloody conflict ended the debate in the United States. All the former Confederate states were forced to ratify the Thirteenth Amendment, which prohibited slavery. The dreams of the leaders of slave rebellions—indeed, of all slaves—had at last been fulfilled.

Chapter Two

The Stono Rebellion

On Sunday, September 9, 1739, a group of about twenty slaves gathered near the Stono Bridge, several miles southwest of Charleston, in the English colony known as South Carolina. They were about to begin an uprising that would become notorious as the largest slave rebellion in the history of the colonies. The rebellion would put complacent white colonists on notice. Henceforth, they would have to be wary of the people they considered their property.

Tensions in the New World

The Stono Rebellion had its roots not just in the slaves' yearning for liberty, but in tensions between the colonial power in the New World. At the time the thirteen American colonies were firmly controlled by Great Britain, although other European powers had also established themselves in North America. France held much of what today is Canada, while Spain claimed Florida as well as a substantial portion of what would become the southwestern United States.

Spain, France, and Great Britain did not coexist peacefully. In Europe the three powers fought wars that spilled over to their North American colonies. As one way of harassing the

St. Augustine: North America's Oldest Settlement

◼

The Stono rebels hoped to reach St. Augustine, Florida, after marching through South Carolina and Georgia. Today, the city is the oldest permanent European settlement on the North American continent. More than forty years before settlers arrived in Jamestown, Virginia, and more than fifty years before the Pilgrims landed in Plymouth, Massachusetts, Spanish settlers made their home in St. Augustine.

Spanish explorer Juan Ponce de León first reached Florida in 1513 and claimed the land for Spain. Over the next fifty years, several Spanish settlement expeditions to Florida failed. In 1564, however, French colonists established a fort in the area, angering the Spanish. In response, Spain's King Philip II organized another expedition in order to colonize the territory and drive out the French. The Spanish expedition arrived off the coast of Florida with six hundred soldiers and settlers on August 28, 1565. The day was the Feast Day of St. Augustine, so the new settlement was named after the saint.

The Spanish eventually destroyed the French fort and forced its settlers out. Soon, however, England began establishing settlements north of Florida. The French established colonies to the west. In response, the Spanish built a strong fort at St. Augustine. They called the fort the Castillo de San Marcos. The fort still stands today, though Spain turned the territory over to the United States after the War of 1812.

Spanish settlers arrive in St. Augustine, Florida.

British, the Spanish encouraged slaves to create trouble for their British masters. Recognizing the importance of slave labor in the southern colonies, the Spanish did what they could to deprive Britain's colonists of that labor. In a royal decree in October 1733, Spain announced that all slaves who fled their masters would be free upon reaching Florida.

To Florida

Spain's bold offer of freedom was most tempting to slaves living in Georgia and South Carolina, the colonies closest to Florida. Some slaves took the Spanish up on their offer of refuge in Florida and fled alone or with one or two companions.

Two slave escapes in 1738 were particularly memorable. In one incident that year, South Carolina slaves passing through Georgia en route to Florida killed several Georgia residents. Then, in November 1738, a band of more than twenty escaped slaves from the colonies arrived in Florida together. The Spanish saw the group's arrival as a perfect opportunity to taunt the British. Spain's government again announced that the Spanish would welcome any slaves who fled to Florida.

The problems posed by restive slaves only worsened for colonists in 1739. In February, there was news that a group of South Carolina slaves had planned to rise up and escape to Florida. None of these rebellions, however, prepared South Carolinians for the Stono uprising later that year.

Timing and the Stono Rebellion

There is no record of who all the participants in the Stono Rebellion were or how long the rebels spent making their plans. Historians also still debate why the Stono rebels chose to begin their insurrection on Sunday, September 9, 1739. The decision was probably based on a number of factors. One likely consideration was that hostilities between Spain and Great Britain finally erupted in September and October, resulting in Great Britain declaring war on Spain. According to historian Peter H. Wood, the news that war had broken out probably reached the Stono area the exact weekend before the uprising began. The news of war alone could have easily triggered a rebellion.

Another factor the rebellious slaves may have weighed was a new South Carolina law called the Security Act. It required all white men to carry a gun to church on Sunday. Whites had long been uneasy about slaves' free hours at the end of the week, when their owners were busy at church. It was one of the few times that slaves were free to gather, and whites therefore recognized it as a time they were vulnerable to attacks. Beginning in the 1720s, South Carolinians wrote several laws requiring whites to be armed on Sundays. These laws were not well enforced, however, so the stricter Security Act was written. It was scheduled to go into effect on September 29, 1739. By rebelling before the law took effect, the slaves may have hoped to attack the planters while many were still unarmed.

Other considerations may have also affected the timing of the insurrection. An epidemic of yellow fever had recently hit Charleston and its surrounding area. The epidemic threw the region into confusion. More than half a dozen Charleston residents were dying each day, and the outbreak was so fierce that much of the city was brought to a halt. The lieutenant governor postponed the meeting of the colonial legislature for more than a month. A school for young ladies shut down. Even the city newspaper, the *Gazette*, stopped printing when its printer fell ill. With many whites sick or dying of this dreaded disease, slaves may have believed it would be easier to revolt.

Liberty!

Whatever their reasons, the rebels chose the morning of September 9 to begin their attack. After gathering at the Stono Bridge, less than 20 miles (32km) from Charleston, the rebel band barged into a nearby store and murdered the two men inside, beheading them and setting their heads on the stairs leading to the building's second floor. Then they ransacked the building, arming themselves with guns and gunpowder, and set out on a road called the Pons Pons.

The road wound from South Carolina through Georgia and on to the port of St. Augustine in Florida. The route totaled more than 250 miles (402km). As the group marched, they called out for others to join them and continued their rampage, plundering and killing as they went. Somehow they obtained two drums and

A fearful runaway slave flees from his captors. In 1733, Spain announced that escaped slaves would be free upon reaching Florida.

a flag, and as they marched they shouted the word "Liberty!" Along the way, the rebels torched homes and stole arms and sometimes liquor.

The rebels did not destroy everything in their path, however. Coming to a tavern, the rebels announced they would not hurt the tavern's owner because he was known to be kind to his slaves. In another instance, a slave hid his master while he convinced the group to leave the man unharmed. Still, after a few hours, the death toll from the rebel army's rampage had grown to more than twenty.

The revolt looked like it might succeed but a fateful encounter waited for the rebels down the road. South Carolina's lieutenant governor, William Bull, and a group of men were returning from the colony's Granville County and riding along the same road as the rebels. At about eleven o'clock that morning, Bull caught sight of the escaped slaves. He immediately realized that the countryside was in the middle of an insurrection. He knew he needed to call for help, fast. Fleeing on horseback with his companions, Bull narrowly escaped capture and alerted the militia.

Meanwhile, the rebels continued their destruction. By afternoon, the rebel brigade had swelled to between sixty and one hundred members. Flush with their success, the group stopped in a field "and set to dancing, Singing and beating Drums, to draw more Negroes to them."[7] according to one report.

Georgia governor General James Oglethorpe offered a reward for the capture of the Stono Rebellion conspirators.

The rebels had traveled 10 miles (16km) from the Stono Bridge. They would not get much farther. At around four in the afternoon, the militia arrived at the field where the slaves were gathered. One hundred armed men confronted the rebels, and a battle ensued. A number of the rebels died on the battlefield. Still others escaped to the woods. According to later reports, "The Negroes were soon routed, though they behaved boldly. . . . Many ran back to their Plantations thinking they had not been missed, but they were there taken and Shot."[8]

Even scattered, the rebels remained dangerous. At least thirty had escaped from the battlefield in small groups. Another thirty were thought to have escaped alone. White citizens feared that the rebels would regroup and renew their destructive march.

As a result, all of South Carolina went on alert. Guards patrolled river crossings and roads. Georgia officials were warned, too, since any rebels still heading for St. Augustine would have to pass through that colony before reaching Spanish territory. In response, Georgia governor General James Oglethorpe dispatched patrols to search for the slaves. He also announced rewards for anyone who caught one of the conspirators. Finally, Oglethorpe called on some allies among the area's Native Americans, asking them to help pursue the rebel slaves.

The Rebels Caught

Within days, the patrols and militia had some success. According to a letter printed in the *Boston Weekly News-Letter*, after two days the militia managed to kill about twenty more rebels and capture another forty. Some rebels were beheaded and their heads set up on posts along the road, a warning to other slaves of the consequences of rebellion. According to the Boston newspaper, other rebels were "shot, some hang'd, and some Gibbeted alive,"[9] meaning they were hung in chains and left to starve, their bodies left hanging even after death.

It took another week, however, for a militia company to catch up with and defeat the largest group of rebels. By that time, the group had managed to march another 30 miles (48km) south. Another month passed before the *News-Letter* finally reported the rebellion over. "The Rebellious [Negroes] are quite [stopped] from doing any further Mischief, many of them having been put to the most cruel Death,"[10] the *News-Letter* reported. In November, a South Carolina Assembly committee recommended that ten Indians who had assisted in the "hunting for, taking and destroying" of "Rebellious Negroes" should be rewarded. They were to be given "a Coat, a Flap, a Hat, a pair of Indian Stockings, a Gun, 2 Pounds [0.9kg] of Powder & 8 Pounds [3.6kg] of Bullets."[11] The insurrection seemed to be over.

Still, some of the uprising's participants were not captured for another six months. One rebel ringleader, whose name was not recorded, eluded capture for three years before being caught and hanged.

Fear in South Carolina

Even with most of the rebels killed or taken prisoner, the fear generated by the slaves' rampage remained strong. A number of farmers near the rebellion route packed up their belongings and families and moved into town. It was safer living close to their neighbors, they reasoned. The number of moves troubled Andrew Leslie, the minister of St. Paul's Parish, where the rebellion began. He worried that if more families left the area he would no longer have anyone to preach to. "I shall have but a Small Congregation at Church,"[12] he wrote in a letter.

Leslie's parishioners were not the only ones who were nervous. A later report summed up the terror the plot had roused: "Every one that had any Relation, any Tie of Nature: every one that had a Life to lose were in the most sensible Manner shocked at such Danger daily hanging over their Heads."[13] With residents fearing another attack, colony officials moved swiftly to prevent future uprisings. In the short term, a special guard was created to patrol the Stono River. Meanwhile, the South Carolina colonial assembly prepared to tighten the planters' control over their slaves.

A New Slave Code

Perhaps the greatest changes that resulted from the Stono Rebellion were new restrictions governing South Carolina's slaves. South Carolina's first slave code, or body of laws governing slaves, had been written in 1696. The code included provisions aimed at preventing crimes by slaves. It also outlined how truant slaves should be tried.

After the Stono Rebellion, the colony's legislators set about writing a new, more stringent slave code. The new provisions became law in May 1740. Called an "Act for the better Ordering and Governing of Negroes and other Slaves," the law's stated purpose was to prevent owners from treating their slaves badly. The colonial legislators reasoned that slaves who were mistreated were more likely to rebel. For this reason, the code prohibited owners from working slaves more than fourteen or fifteen hours a day. Furthermore, owners who forced their slaves to work on Sunday could be fined. Finally, if slave owners refused to give their slaves sufficient clothing or food, a complaint could be filed with authorities on behalf of the slaves.

Warrior Rebels?

The Stono rebels seized guns, attracted more slaves to their rebellion, and fought well. What made them so successful?

Historian John K. Thornton has one theory. He believes that the Stono rebels could have been Kongolese warriors before being taken to the United States as slaves. That would help explain their success. Several pieces of evidence suggest that the rebels were warriors: their country of origin, their skill with guns, and their battlefield tactics.

To begin, sources writing soon after the rebellion say that the rebels were African-born. Thornton argues that based on slave trade patterns the rebels likely came from Kongo, today the Democratic Republic of the Congo. If that is the case, the chance that the rebels were former warriors increases dramatically. Beginning in 1665 and continuing for the next four decades, civil wars raged in the Kongo. Soldiers captured in battle were often sold as slaves, and many of the slaves coming from the Kongo were former soldiers.

The weapons that the rebels chose also mark them as likely warriors. To begin their attack, the rebels armed themselves with guns, which they apparently handled well, sources say. Accurately shooting a gun, however, takes practice, and firing a gun was not a skill that the rebels learned in America, where laws kept guns out of slaves' hands. African warriors of the period, however, were increasingly familiar with guns, which Europeans traded for African slaves or goods.

Finally, the rebels' battle tactics also suggest that they had been soldiers. Primary sources say that after the rebels' initial attack they began dancing in a field. This is a distinctly African practice. Soldiers prepared for war by dancing to sharpen their reflexes. In fact, dancing in preparation for war was so common in Kongo that *dancing a war dance* was often used as a synonym for *declaring war*, according to Thornton. Moreover, when the militia arrived, the slaves fought a brief skirmish and fled. Some of the groups that fled together then fought subsequent skirmishes. This was a typical battle pattern in Africa—a series of short fights.

Despite such seemingly generous provisions, the new legislation's aim was really to tighten restrictions on slaves themselves. The law prohibited slaves from assembling in groups, buying liquor, or carrying a gun without their owner's permission. No group of more than seven slaves was allowed to travel from one location to another unless a white person accompanied them. Any white person who spotted such a group traveling unaccompanied was authorized to "apprehend all and every such slaves, and shall and may whip them, not exceeding twenty lashes on the bare back."[14]

The act also set out a series of fines, punishments, and rewards designed to keep whites in control of their slaves. Any white person who taught a slave to read, for example, faced a fine of one hundred pounds. Any slave who assaulted a white person could be killed. And anyone who apprehended fugitive slaves fleeing to Spanish territory would be rewarded with a bounty of between five and one hundred pounds depending on the gender and age of the runaways, where they were captured, and if they were taken dead or alive.

The law also mentioned the Stono Rebellion specifically, exonerating any white militiaman or citizen who had killed slaves during the rebellion. The killings were justified in the name of preserving safety. Not all the provisions of the slave code were ever enforced, but that they were enacted attests to the fear that the uprising evoked among the colonists.

Restrictions Mount

The legislature did not stop with enacting a tougher slave code. The colonial lawmakers also strengthened South Carolina's Patrol Act in 1740, the same year that the new slave code was passed. Patrols were one way slave owners made sure their slaves were not plotting against them. On weekly rounds, patrol members watched for runaways and slaves acting suspiciously. Patrol members could stop and question slaves, search slave quarters, and punish slaves with whippings. The legislators also increased the number of people who were required to do patrol duty. The new law also divided up districts into smaller "beats" that were easier to patrol and imposed fines on whites who neglected their patrol duties. The lawmakers hoped that more and more thorough patrols would make it more difficult for slaves to plan another uprising. These tougher provisions clearly were written with the Stono Rebellion in mind. Certainly, if a patrol had caught the rebels when they first assembled at the bridge, they never would have begun their murderous rampage.

In the wake of the Stono Rebellion, the assembly also attempted to limit the number of slaves imported into South Carolina from outside of North America. Planters believed that newly imported slaves, remembering the freedom they had lost, were

"My Kinsman, Cato"

In the 1930s a writer employed by the U.S. government to preserve oral history spoke with an African American man named George Cato. Cato said he was descended from the leader of the Stono Rebellion, whose name he said was also Cato. He told the interviewer:

> My granddaddy was a son of de son of de Stono slave commander. He say his daddy often take him over de route of de rebel slave march, dat time when dere was sho' big trouble all 'bout dat neighborhood. As it come down to me, I thinks de first Cato take a darin' chance on losin' his life, not so much for his own benefit as it was to help others. He was not lak some slaves, much 'bused by deir masters. My kinsfolks not 'bused. . . . Cato was teached how to read and write by his rich master.

> How it all start? Dat what I ask but nobody ever tell me how 100 slaves between de Combahee and Edisto rivers come to meet in de woods not far from de Stono River on September 9, 1739. And how they elect a leader, my kinsman, Cato, and late dat day march to Stono town, break in a warehouse, kill two white men in charge, and take all de guns and ammunition they wants. But they do it, wid dis start, they turn south and march on.

> They work fast, coverin' 15 miles [24 km], passin' many fine plantations, and in every single case, stop, and break in de house and kill men, women, and children. Then they take what they want, 'cludin' arms, clothes, liquor and food.

Quoted in Mark M. Smith, *Stono: Documenting and Interpreting a Southern Slave Revolt.* Columbia: University of South Carolina Press, 2005, p. 56.

more likely to rebel than those who had grown up in the colony. In fact, there is some evidence that the leaders of the Stono Rebellion were born in Africa. In an effort to decrease that number of foreign-born slaves, the legislature imposed high taxes on anyone who brought slaves in from outside the country.

From the new slave code to the new patrol act, the Stono Rebellion changed slavery in South Carolina. Masters became increasingly concerned about what keeping slaves meant in terms of their personal safety. They recognized that the potential for rebellion existed every day. One man, looking back at the Stono uprising, wrote that now "the inhabitants cannot live without perpetually guarding their own Safety."[15]

Chapter Three

Gabriel's Rebellion

The year 1776 was a year of revolution in America. Colonists, angry over taxes imposed by their British rulers, rebelled against the government and loudly proclaimed their independence. That same year, another revolutionary was born to a slave family in Virginia. The boy, known as Gabriel, would grow up to plan a slave rebellion of a size and scale unimagined by white citizens at the time. The rhetoric of liberty so passionately proclaimed by American revolutionaries was seen in a very different light by whites when it inspired a black man to speak out on behalf of his fellow slaves.

Born on a Tobacco Plantation

Gabriel was born on the plantation of Thomas Henry Prosser, a wealthy Virginia tobacco farmer. Prosser owned a large estate called Brookfield in Henrico County, 6 miles (9.7km) north of Richmond. At the time Gabriel was born in 1776, Prosser owned more than fifty slaves, including Gabriel's parents and two older brothers. Gabriel's brother Martin worked as a field hand. Gabriel and his other brother Solomon were trained as blacksmiths, which may have been the occupation of Gabriel's father— although the records made at the time are unclear on this.

Workers tend to a tobacco field in colonial Virginia. The slave known as Gabriel was born on a tobacco farm in 1776.

Gabriel's skill as a blacksmith gave him advantages that most of his fellow slaves could only dream of. Most plantation owners lacked the luxury of being able to spare a slave to do skilled work, and white artisans needed skilled help. Thomas Prosser therefore allowed Gabriel to hire out, or work for others, when he was not needed on the plantation. As a consequence, Gabriel spent at least several days every month away from the plantation, working in Richmond. Being away from the direct supervision of his master and plantation overseers gave Gabriel a taste of what it might be like to be free. In addition, although most of what he earned went to Prosser, hiring out meant that Gabriel could keep a small portion of his pay.

Working in Richmond expanded Gabriel's limited horizons. City life and plantation life were very different. In the city, Gabriel worked with white laborers and met other black artisans. After work, white and black laborers often drank and talked together. Their conversations frequently turned to politics and other news gleaned from the newspapers. Gabriel also met black men and women who had managed to purchase their freedom, a circumstance that any slave envied. No doubt, these free blacks served as an example for Gabriel of what he might do with the wages he was allowed to keep.

Hog Stealing Lands Gabriel in Court

Whatever Gabriel might have thought of his prospects for freedom, events in September 1799 provided him with motives for plotting rebellion. That month, Gabriel, his brother Solomon, and a slave named Jupiter, who lived on another plantation, were caught stealing a pig from a neighboring farm belonging to a man named Absalom Johnson. Pig stealing by slaves was not uncommon, but when Johnson caught the men he became furious. Confronted by the irate farmer, Gabriel fought back. He knocked Johnson to the ground and scuffled with him. During the fight, Gabriel bit off a large part of Johnson's left ear.

Stealing a white man's property was no small matter, but assaulting a white man was a serious crime. All three slaves were quickly taken before the city's slave court, known officially as the court of oyer and terminer.

On September 23, the court's five justices found Jupiter guilty of "hogstealing" and sentenced him to receive thirty-nine lashes at the public whipping post. Solomon was tried next. Johnson told the court that he was afraid that Solomon, who had threatened him during the fight, might try to retaliate by setting fire to his property. But Solomon convinced the justices that he was not dangerous, and they let him go.

Two weeks later, it was Gabriel who faced the court. The justices saw Johnson's mangled ear and listened as he described the fight, and Gabriel was quickly found guilty. He could have been sentenced to death, but his knowledge of the Bible saved him from the gallows. Under a 1792 statute, slaves who were able to recite a verse from the Bible could have their sentences reduced. This was called "benefit of clergy." Gabriel, whose parents had raised him in their Christian faith, was able to recite a verse and the justices therefore ordered that he be branded on his left hand as punishment for his crimes. Not only was this a painful and public humiliation, but if Gabriel was ever convicted of a similar offense, the brand would signal that he was ineligible for a reduced sentence. If Gabriel lost his temper again, he could lose his life.

Rebellion on His Mind

The sentence was soon carried out. Humiliated and angry at the outcome of his trial, Gabriel almost certainly would have yearned all the more for freedom. Gabriel could have tried to run away as many other slaves did, but the man who had grown up amid the rhetoric of liberty for all was about to make freedom for himself and his fellow slaves his mission.

Two events in particular were likely on Gabriel's mind as he plotted rebellion: a successful slave uprising on the French island of Saint Domingue and the tense political atmosphere that provided a backdrop to rebellion. First, Gabriel would have been well aware of a slave rebellion that had taken place on Saint Domingue in 1791. When Gabriel was just fifteen, a slave named Toussaint L'Ouverture helped lead a rebellion there, and by 1793 the slaves controlled much of the colony. Gabriel probably heard reports of the successful rebellion through his contacts with white artisans who had access to newspapers. In addition, white Dominguan refugees had fled to Virginia in large numbers with their slaves, who spread the story. News that other slaves had won their freedom through rebellion impressed and inspired Gabriel.

By 1799 Gabriel was also aware of a growing split in the country. As a result of his trips to Richmond and his conversations with white artisans. Gabriel knew there was a growing divide between the country's two main political factions. On one side were the Democratic-Republicans, who wanted states to be largely autonomous and the role of the national government limited; on the other side were the Federalists, who wanted a strong and powerful central government. Tensions between the parties over a variety of other issues were also reaching a fever pitch with an upcoming presidential election. There was even widespread talk that the country might break into civil war. Gabriel would have hoped to use this divide to his advantage.

Gabriel believed that once the revolt began, others, including some disaffected whites, would join his struggle for liberty. He had reason to believe that Republican artisans, like those he had

Toussaint L'Ouverture's slave rebellion on the French island of Saint Domingue inspired Gabriel to lead his own uprising in Virginia.

worked with in Richmond, would see his struggle for liberty as similar to their own struggle against Federalists. Gabriel hoped that with wide support he could convince state authorities to free the slaves once and for all.

Readying for Rebellion

Inspired by the Dominguan rebellion and believing the country to be on the verge of civil war, Gabriel began mapping out his uprising. He reasoned that a small but well-armed band could enter Richmond in the dead of night and take control of the city's armory. After seizing weapons and gaining wider support, the rebels would force white town leaders to give them their freedom. To put his plan into motion, however, Gabriel needed recruits.

Some of Gabriel's first co-conspirators were his brother Solomon and another Prosser slave known only as Ben. From there, the conspiracy grew. As blacksmiths who hired out, Solomon and Gabriel could easily gain access to others and talk about the plot. Some of the other slaves they recruited, like Ben Woolfolk and Sam Byrd Jr., also hired out to nearby counties like Caroline and Hanover. There they were able to recruit still more men. Slave gatherings, which routinely took place on Saturday evenings and Sundays, provided another opportunity to sign up rebels. Conspirators often attended gatherings at Henrico County's Brook Bridge, where slaves congregated on weekends for picnics and religious services.

Gabriel (pictured in this drawing) gained immense support from his brother and other slaves.

News of the plot spread and the size of the rebel force grew quickly. One person later said that at this point the plot counted two thousand rebels. Others put the number at six or even ten thousand. Some believed that slaves in North Carolina were involved. And the governor of Mississippi Territory later reported the plot had involved fifty thousand. Virginia governor James Monroe was more reserved in his estimates, but acknowledged:

It was distinctly seen that [the plot] embraced most of the slaves in this city [Richmond] and [neighborhood], and that the combination extended to several of the adjacent counties, Hanover, Caroline, Louisa, Chesterfield, and to the [neighborhood] of the Point of the Fork; and there was good cause to believe that the knowledge of such a project pervaded other parts, if not the whole of the State.[16]

As the plot grew, Gabriel and his brother Solomon gathered weapons. Slaves stole scythes they used for work in the fields, and the two blacksmiths reworked them. By breaking the blades in half, sharpening them, and fastening them into handles, Gabriel and Solomon made weapons that, although crude, were sharp enough to sever a man's arm with one blow. Other slaves stole and hid what weapons they could, including crossbows, swords, and clubs.

A Detailed Plan

By August 1800 Gabriel was ready to reveal the final details of his plan to his followers. His plot called for slaves from the Brookfield plantation to first kill their master, Thomas Prosser. Then they would go to a neighboring farm and kill Absalom Johnson, the man who had caught Gabriel and his companions stealing his hog. Those tasks completed, the rebels would rendezvous with recruits from other counties at nearby Brook Bridge, 6 miles (9.7km) due north of Richmond. From there, Gabriel would lead one hundred men in storming a nearby tavern where arms were stored. Then, it would be on to Richmond.

As the rebels approached the city, the plan called for them to divide into three units. One group would set fire to warehouses in the upper part of town as a diversion. A second group would attack the penitentiary, where Gabriel knew a large supply of gunpowder was stored. The final group, led by Gabriel himself, would take the capitol building and appropriate its stash of guns. At some point Gabriel also planned to take Governor James Monroe hostage. Gabriel hoped that the governor would be willing to negotiate with him and his fellow slaves for their freedom.

While they marched, Gabriel planned to fly a banner inscribed with the words "death or Liberty." The inscription was a play on the words of a famous Virginia patriot, Patrick Henry, who on the eve of the Revolutionary War had proclaimed, "Give me liberty or give me death."

Gabriel did not know how Richmond's citizens would react to his invasion. He hoped they would sympathize with the rebels rather than oppose them. As one rebel explained later, "if the white people agreed to their freedom they would then hoist a white flag, and [Gabriel] would dine and drink with the merchants of the city on the day when it should be agreed to."[17]

Rain Delays the Rebellion

Gabriel planned his rebellion for the evening of Saturday, August 30. Scheduling the uprising for a Saturday made sense. Traditionally, slaves worked only half of the day on Saturday. Then, if they got permission from their masters, many headed to the city. White citizens therefore, would not be suspicious of a large group of black men heading into town on a Saturday. Word was sent to other rebel groups to ready themselves for action that day.

Just around sunset on August 30, however, nature interfered with Gabriel's plans. The sky darkened, and a massive downpour began. Journalist James Callender recorded the event. He wrote, "there came on the most terrible thunder Storm, accompanied with an enormous rain, that I ever witnessed in this State."[18] The heavy rain flooded creeks and the rising waters washed out bridges. Travel was nearly impossible as a result. It is unclear how many wet and muddy rebels actually made it to the rendezvous point that night, but it did not matter. With their path impassable and their numbers small, Gabriel called off the insurrection.

The Plot Unravels

Even after the storm ruined the rebels' plans, Gabriel hoped his rebellion could be salvaged. He scheduled a meeting of his followers for the following night. But the rain had had another negative effect on Gabriel's plans. As the downpour raged, a twenty-seven-year-old slave named Pharoah, a recent recruit to the uprising, began to have doubts about the plan. Pharoah worked on a small farm near Brookfield, and because of the farm's small size, he had close contact with his master, Mosby Sheppard. Historians speculate that the two likely worked together in the fields, so Pharoah would have felt a closeness to Sheppard that was uncommon between a master and slaves on a large plantation.

Political Perils of 1800

———————— ■ ————————

The Federalists and the Democratic-Republicans were the first two political parties in the United States. Like political parties today, the groups disagreed on many issues. By 1800 these disagreements were at a boiling point. To Gabriel, it probably seemed that the Union was falling apart, and he hoped to exploit this rift with his rebellion.

In fact, there were many reasons for tension between the two parties. First, there were fundamental differences in their beliefs. The Federalists—led by Alexander Hamilton and John Adams—favored a strong central government, strong army, and loose interpretation of the Constitution. The Democratic-Republicans—led by Thomas Jefferson and James Madison—believed in the opposite. They supported a weak central government, states' rights, and a strict interpretation of the Constitution. And while the Federalists supported Britain, the United States' former colonial ruler, Democratic-Republicans saw France as the most important U.S. ally.

In 1798 these differences reached a crisis point. Federalists in Congress passed the Alien and Sedition Acts, which were signed into law by President John Adams. The acts, which made it illegal to criticize the government, were a direct attack on Democratic-Republicans. In response, James Madison and Thomas Jefferson anonymously wrote the Virginia and Kentucky Resolutions, attacking the acts and challenging the authority of the federal government.

The angry exchanges between the parties escalated further in 1800, an election year and the year of Gabriel's rebellion. The 1800 campaigns were some of the most heated and malicious in the nation's history. Federalist newspapers called Jefferson an atheist and accused him of treason for opposing the Alien and Sedition Acts. One Federalist newspaper warned that if Jefferson won there would be a civil war. Republicans, meanwhile, called Adams a fool and a tyrant. In some regions the party organized militias in case of war.

With all this fierce rhetoric, it is not surprising that Gabriel thought others would be willing to challenge the government alongside him.

Reflecting on his situation, Pharoah saw that revealing what he knew about the plot could help him. If he told his owner about the planned uprising, Sheppard might reward him by allowing him to purchase his freedom at a very low price.

Pharoah decided to reveal what he knew, and his surprised master alerted his neighbors. Before long, groups of armed whites were patrolling the area, detaining any black man whose behavior they found suspicious. By Sunday afternoon, Governor James Monroe had received word of the plot. With patrols blanketing the area, the rebels quickly understood that their secret had been betrayed and discovered. Some of the conspirators attempted to hide. Others tried to escape. Gabriel himself eluded authorities and fled Henrico County.

Captures and the Court

Government officials eventually recognized the vast size of the failed plot and began jailing suspected rebels in earnest. Guards lined the road to Richmond, and soldiers patrolled the capital. As news of the uprising spread, terrified citizens all over the state demanded protection. Governor Monroe called out the state militia. Every militia commander in the state was notified, and over 650 men were called into service. Soon, Richmond's jail was crowded with accused conspirators.

Locked in the city's jail, most of the captives simply glared at their jailers and said nothing about the plot. Ben, the Prosser slave who had been one of the earliest recruits, was an exception. He was one of the youngest rebels, and because he had been brought into the conspiracy early on, he knew most of the details. Scared for his life, Ben made a deal with the authorities. If he testified against other conspirators, he would not be punished.

With Ben as a key witness, trials for the accused rebels

The Court of Oyer and Terminer

—■—

From the late 1600s to the Civil War, slaves accused of committing a crime in Virginia and many other states were tried before a special court called a court of oyer and terminer. Its name literally means "to hear and determine" or decide. In Virginia, this type of court was established by a 1692 law. When this type of court convened, at least five justices heard the case. Then they collectively pronounced a sentence. While the accused slaves were provided with a lawyer, there was no jury, and the court had absolute say over life and death. Only the governor could overrule a sentence pronounced by the court. White slave owners saw this system as fair. Many slaves realized they had little chance of a fair trial in this type of court.

began in Richmond on September 11, 1800. The men were tried in the same courthouse where Gabriel had been tried for stealing the hog, One by one, the rebels faced the court of oyer and ter-miner, with Ben and Mosby Sheppard's Pharoah testifying against them. Eventually, other slaves broke down, hoping their testimo-ny would get them lighter sentences. The accused were allowed to speak in their own defense, but their words rarely did them much good. One rebel, asked what he had to say to the court, defended his actions by citing the example of America's founders:

> I have nothing more to offer than what General Washing-ton would have had to offer, had he been taken by the British and put to trial by them. I have adventured my life in [endeavoring] to obtain the liberty of my countrymen, and am a willing sacrifice to their cause: and I beg, as a [favor], that I may be immediately led to execution. I know that you have pre-determined to shed my blood, why then all this mockery of a trial?[19]

By early October, more than twenty rebels had been found guilty and sentenced to hang. Their executions, staged in various locations throughout the county, were meant as a warning to other slaves who might be thinking of rebellion. Still, the one rebel that officials wanted most still eluded their grasp—Gabriel.

Gabriel on the Gallows

As soon as Gabriel had realized that his plot could not be saved, he had fled Henrico County, probably along the swampy Chick-ahominy River. Two weeks later, he had reached the James River, 4 miles (6.4 km) downstream from Richmond. Anchored off-shore was the schooner *Mary*, and Gabriel decided to try his luck gaining passage on the ship. After hailing and boarding the ship, he told the captain he was a free man headed for Norfolk, where the ship was also bound.

Gabriel had no papers identifying him as free, and two slaves aboard the *Mary* who had worked in the area told the captain they recognized Gabriel as the rebel leader. But the captain, either doubting the slaves or sympathizing with Gabriel, merely set sail for Norfolk.

Still, Gabriel was not safe. Authorities offered a $300 award for any member of the conspiracy willing to turn in their leader. That sum was nearly enough to buy a slave's freedom. Billy, one of the slaves aboard the *Mary*, decided he wanted the reward.

When the ship docked in Norfolk a week later, Billy informed police that Gabriel was aboard, and Norfolk officials stormed onto the vessel. Newspapers reported. "Without delay the Villon was arrested" but Gabriel "manifested the greatest of firmness and composure, [showing] not the least disposition to equivocate or [screen] himself from justice."[20] Ironically, because Billy had not been part of the conspiracy, he received only a small portion of the reward money.

Returned to Richmond in chains, Gabriel was brought before the court of oyer and terminer on October 6. Outside the courthouse, many whites gathered to jeer, while some slaves and free blacks waited quietly to learn Gabriel's fate. Inside, Ben Woolfolk and Prosser's Ben testified against their leader. After hearing the two slaves detail the plan of the rebellion, the court unanimously found Gabriel guilty. He was sentenced to hang the following morning. Though Gabriel had faced the court in stony silence during his trial, his expression changed when he heard his sentence. Some observers believed he wanted to confess. Instead, Gabriel brazenly asked the court to delay his hanging. He wanted to die on October 10, alongside several other rebels. The court agreed to this request.

Officials may have accommodated Gabriel in the hopes that he would reveal more details of the plot, but he refused. On October 10, 1800, after hanging several other rebels, officials brought Gabriel to the town gallows at the corner of Fifteenth and Broad in Richmond. "I do hearby certify," recorded slave owner Mosby Sheppard, "that the within mentioned Slave [Gabriel] was executed agreeably to the within [Sentence] of the Court."[21]

Gabriel's Legacy

Ultimately, twenty-seven men paid for their involvement in the conspiracy with their lives. Other participants were pardoned but sold to traders who agreed to transport and sell them outside the United States. Selling the slaves far away from their families served as a punishment and had the additional advantage of

"Where to Stay the Hand of the Executioner"

■

As the governor of Virginia, James Monroe was deeply involved in the aftermath of Gabriel's rebellion. He assured citizens of their safety, stationed troops, and monitored the rebels' trials. But as the number of rebels being hanged mounted, Monroe wrote to his old friend Thomas Jefferson for advice. Ten of the rebels had been executed, Monroe wrote Jefferson on September 15, 1800. He believed another twenty or forty would be tried and found guilty. With more rebels still on the loose, Monroe worried about the growing number of executions. He wrote, "when to arrest the hand of the Executioner is a question of great importance." Was "mercy or severity . . . the better policy in this case"? What, he asked, did Jefferson think?

Jefferson responded on September 20. "Where to stay the hand of the executioner is an important question," he wrote his friend. Jefferson understood that worried citizens might want the executions to continue. But, he wrote, "there is a strong sentiment that there has been hanging enough. The other states & the world at large will forever condemn us if we indulge a principle of revenge, or go one step beyond absolute necessity. . . . Our situation is indeed a difficult one: for I doubt whether these people can ever be permitted to go at large among us with safety."

Soon after receiving Jefferson's response, Monroe began pardoning some of the conspirators.

Quoted in Douglas R. Egerton, *Gabriel's Rebellion*. Chapel Hill: University of North Carolina Press, 1993, p. 89.

Thomas Jefferson to James Monroe, September 20, 1800. *The Thomas Jefferson Papers*. http://memory.loc.gov/ammem/collections/jefferson_papers.

removing proven troublemakers from U.S. territory. Gabriel's rebellion had failed, but the plot had a lasting effect. His bold plans inspired other slaves and worried Virginia leaders. Not long after the hangings and trials of 1800 concluded, a slave named Sancho rekindled plans for a slave uprising. Sancho was a ferryman who worked the rivers of Virginia. He planned a rebellion for around Easter 1802, spreading news of his plot through his contacts with other watermen. Less well organized than Gabriel's plot, the rebellion was discovered before it got off the ground. Twenty-five slaves from Virginia and North Carolina were hanged for their role in the conspiracy.

The rebellions of 1800 and 1802 both had a lasting effect on the government of Virginia. Before Gabriel's rebellion, government leaders had been complacent. They could not believe their slaves could or would rebel. In the plot's aftermath, many recognized that had it not rained, the uprising would have proceeded, with deadly consequences. Journalist James Callender was blunt in his assessment of the rebels' strength. He wrote to Thomas Jefferson that the rebels "could hardly have failed of success" because "after all, we only could muster four or five hundred men of whom not more than thirty had Muskets." [22]

When the Virginia legislature opened its new session in December 1800, Governor Monroe gave legislators a full report on the rebellion. In response, the legislature passed two laws, strengthening the state militia and the patrol system. Gabriel's rebellion also prompted legislators to think seriously about the system of slavery. For several years after the rebellion, the legislature explored the possibility of colonization, purchasing land overseas where slaves could be sent to live.

While the debates ultimately amounted to nothing, Virginians had begun to recognize slavery's inherent problems. Though the legislators could not agree what to do about slavery, Gabriel's rebellion showed them that if slavery were to continue in Virginia, slave owners could no longer be lax about enforcing restrictions. Slave owners would have to control their slaves using an increasingly restrictive system.

Chapter Four

Denmark Vesey's Rebellion

Denmark Vesey, a carpenter living in Charleston, South Carolina, was an unlikely leader of a slave rebellion. Although he was born a slave, Vesey purchased his freedom in 1799. He had made enough money to rent a home, and by the time he began plotting rebellion he was in his fifties. But despite being an established, free member of society, Vesey was not content. Working through Charleston's African church, Vesey recruited a group of followers and plotted a rebellion that, had it succeeded, would have meant freedom for perhaps nine thousand slaves.

Denmark

Denmark Vesey's early life is somewhat of a mystery. Historians speculate that he was born about 1767. It is possible he was born in Africa, but it is more likely he was born to slave parents on the island of St. Thomas in the Caribbean. What is certain is that by 1781 a slave named Denmark was a teenager living on the island. That year, a thirty-four-year-old slave trader and ship's captain named Joseph Vesey visited St. Thomas. Vesey made a living transporting goods and slaves. When he arrived on St. Thomas, he bought 400 slaves, including Denmark. Vesey then transported the slaves to the island of Saint

A slave gazes at Charleston, South Carolina from a church tower. Denmark Vesey organized a slave rebellion with help from his Charleston church.

Domingue, where he sold them and they were put to work in the fields.

Soon after he arrived on Saint Domingue, however, Denmark began having epileptic seizures. No one knows whether these episodes were real or faked by the teenager, but when Captain Vesey next returned to the island, Denmark's owner demanded his money back. The slave was unfit, Vesey was told.

Captain Vesey gave the slave owner his money back, and Denmark became the captain's personal servant. For the next two years, Denmark traveled with the captain on his trade route as he purchased slaves in Africa and transported them across the Atlantic Ocean. By 1783, however, the captain wanted to settle down. He chose Charleston, South Carolina, as his new home.

Two Life Changes

Denmark's life changed drastically when he arrived in Charleston with his owner. The city was a busy port, and Captain Vesey quickly established a business importing goods and slaves. In his new business, Captain Vesey needed Denmark less, so he allowed his slave to hire out his time and labor. This meant that Denmark was paid to work for others. Most of Denmark's earnings went to Vesey, but some of the money was his to keep.

In the fall of 1799, Denmark purchased a ticket in the East-Bay Lottery with money he had earned hiring out. That ticket changed his life. When the winning lottery numbers were published, Denmark was shocked to see that he had won $1,500. That was more money than a slave could save in ten years. It was also more than enough to buy his freedom. On December 31, 1799, after turning over $600 of his winnings to Captain Vesey, Denmark walked down the streets of Charleston a free man.

Free at Last

For the next two decades, Denmark led a quiet and unremarkable life in Charleston. He worked as a carpenter, a skill he probably learned through an apprenticeship with a local craftsman. Even after winning the lottery and his freedom, things were hard for the former slave. Though free, he did not have the same privileges as whites, and in some ways he was still treated as a slave. City ordinances limited the amount of money free blacks could make per day and the jobs they could hold. Free blacks had to pay taxes not imposed on whites; they were tried in slave courts if they ever committed a crime. Vesey also lived with an ever-present, well-founded fear of being kidnapped and sold back into slavery. Until the mid-1800s there were no laws against kidnapping free blacks and selling them back into slavery.

During the first years after he purchased his freedom, Denmark began to read extensively. Captain Vesey had taught his slave to read, and now Denmark read any antislavery book and pamphlet he could get his hands on. He constantly studied the Bible, especially the Old Testament, and was fascinated by passages that referred to slavery.

Vesey also attended church regularly. Around 1818, Vesey joined or helped found a new church in Charleston. It was a branch of the African Methodist Episcopal (AME) church. Unlike the church he had previously belonged to, the AME church had only black congregants. Vesey became a class leader—that is, a layperson who taught Bible lessons during the week. The church and Vesey's class meetings would eventually play a central part in his plans for rebellion.

The Conspirators

Denmark Vesey may have been free, but he hated the fact that others were still enslaved. By 1821, and perhaps as early as 1817, Vesey began plotting a rebellion that would end this injustice. Vesey knew that for his plans to work he would need help. He needed lieutenants—men who could collect weapons, obtain donations, and recruit followers. Vesey chose his closest conspirators carefully. He wanted men who were respected by the black community, and he needed at least some who were living away from their owners. This would allow them to travel and recruit other rebels more readily.

Some of Vesey's first lieutenants were friends and fellow members of the AME church. Peter Poyas, a ship's carpenter, was one logical choice. He was a good friend and able to read and write. This allowed him to keep lists of recruits. Another literate slave, Jack Glenn, collected money from slaves to be used to purchase supplies for the rebellion. Also part of Vesey's inner circle were Monday Gell, a harness maker who lived away from his master, and Rolla and Ned Bennett, slaves belonging to South Carolina's governor, Thomas Bennett. Bennett's slaves promised to kill the governor when the rebellion began.

Finally, Vesey selected Jack Prichard as a lieutenant. Around Charleston, Prichard was known as "Gullah Jack" because he understood and could speak Gullah, a mixture of English and African languages spoken by slaves on the Sea Islands of South Carolina and Georgia. Gullah Jack brought something to the rebellion that none of the other conspirators did: He was said to

The Rebel Church

Charleston's African Methodist Episcopal (AME) church played an important part in Denmark Vesey's rebellion. Many of Vesey's lieutenants were friends from church, and Bible study meetings he led often turned into planning sessions for the rebellion.

It is fitting that the AME church was central to the rebellion because its creation was an act of defiance itself. In 1817, after Charleston's Methodist church took away their right to meet separately, more than four thousand slaves and free blacks quit the church and formed their own congregation. Though a white monitor was present at all services, all the church's parishioners were black, and the church was one of the first all-black churches in the nation. Charleston's black church grew so quickly that soon a second church had to be built to accommodate worshippers. Denmark Vesey became a member of the second church and taught Bible lessons during the week. His fiery lessons often discussed slavery in the Bible, and these sessions later evolved into secret meetings for the rebels.

Vesey's church was rebuilt after Charleston officials had it torn down in 1822.

William Paul, who testified against the accused rebels, said during their trials that the whole church was part of the plot. This is probably an exaggeration, but it was true that many blacks accused of being part of the insurrection attended the church. As a result, the African church quickly became the target of white anger. Soon after the rebellion, the church's ministers were given fifteen days to pack up their belongings and leave Charleston, and, under pressure, the congregations dissolved. In 1822 city officials demolished the congregation's main building.

have been a priest in Africa and a conjurer. It was a position that brought him both respect and fear. Members of the black community believed that he had special powers and that he was invincible. With his help, many believed, the rebellion was sure to succeed.

Nighttime Plotting

At nighttime meetings in his home in Charleston, Vesey and his lieutenants refined the details of their plot. As the city bells tolled midnight on the night planned for the uprising, slaves would kill their masters as they slept. Rolla Bennett would murder both the governor and the mayor, the objective being to throw the city into confusion. Then house servants and slaves from the countryside would head into the streets. One group would seize the city's arsenal. Another rebel band would set fires and begin killing white inhabitants. Denmark Vesey and his men would capture the city's guardhouse from the men who served as the night watch. What was to happen then is uncertain. Once they took control of the city, Vesey and his band may have intended to take over ships in the harbor and sail to Saint Domingue, where slaves had succeeded on wresting control from their owners.

With the groundwork laid, Vesey's main conspirators and a handful of other recruiters began approaching other slaves about the rebellion. One important recruiting ground was the AME church. The Bible sessions Vesey taught at his home often focused on slavery in the Bible, and meetings quickly turned into discussions of rebellion as one means of striking a blow against slavery.

Inside and outside of church, Vesey and his recruiters knew they had to be careful about whom they approached. They wanted to make sure the potential recruits would not alert authorities to the plot. Vesey suggested concentrating on slaves who appeared unhappy with their masters, since they were most likely to rebel and not tip off their owners. He also warned recruiters about approaching house servants since these slaves were generally closer to their masters than field hands were. Selecting the recruits was crucial; if even one was disloyal, the entire plan could be ruined.

As their forces grew, the rebels began to gather weapons. One participant stole a bullet mold, which the conspirators used to form bullets. Then they hid supplies of bullets around the city. A blacksmith recruited to the plot made and hid one hundred pikes, long wooden poles with one end sharpened. Denmark himself purchased some wigs from a barber. By painting their faces white and wearing the wigs, Vesey hoped that in the dark he and some of his rebels would be mistaken by any night patrols for white men. Recruits from the country were asked to bring any available object that could serve as a weapon—hoes, axes, and other farming tools.

By May, word of the planned rebellion was widespread in slave quarters. Officials who later tried to determine the extent of the conspiracy could say only that "it extended to the north of Charleston many miles towards Santee, and unquestionably into St. John's Parish, to the south to James' and John's Islands, and to the west beyond Bacon's Bridge over Ashley River."[23] Denmark Vesey himself was later said to have traveled 70 to 80 miles (113 to 129km) from the city to recruit followers. Some historians estimate that nine thousand individuals knew about the plot.

A Fatal Mistake

Vesey planned his rebellion for July 1822. Events in May, however, made him change his plans abruptly. On the afternoon of Saturday, May 25, one of Vesey's recruiters made a deadly mistake. Walking down the wharf below the city's fish market, recruiter William Paul approached a slave who was alone. William Paul first mentioned a ship the two could see out in the harbor. Then he changed topics.

The slave, Peter Prioleau, later told city authorities:

> After some trifling conversation [about the ship], he remarked with considerable earnestness to me. Do you know that something serious is about to take place? To which I replied no. Well, said he, there is, and many of us are determined to right ourselves! I asked him to explain himself—when he remarked, why, we are determined to shake off our bondage, and for this purpose we stand on a good foundation, many have joined, and if you will go with me, I will show you the man, who has the list of names who will take yours down.[24]

Peter Prioleau, however, wanted no part in any rebellion. He was a house servant and devoted to his owner, Colonel John

Pictured is Denmark Vesey's house. Vesey's plan nearly unraveled after Charleston authorities questioned some of the conspirators.

Prioleau. Peter's master was away the day he was approached at the wharf, but as soon as John Prioleau returned on May 30, Peter alerted him to the plot. That afternoon, Colonel Prioleau took Peter to the mayor's house. There, Peter repeated his story for Governor Thomas Bennett, Charleston mayor James Hamilton, and members of the city council. Because of Peter's accusations, the officials called in William Paul, the man who had approached Prioleau at the wharf. The entire plot was now in danger.

Good Acting Salvages the Plot

Initially, William claimed he knew nothing about a rebellion. After being threatened with torture and confined in the city's workhouse, where slaves were sent for whippings and other punishments, he broke down. William said Ned Bennett, Peter Poyas, and a man named Mingo Harth were involved in the conspiracy, and the officials summoned Poyas and Harth. Fortunately for the conspirators, the two were good actors. Told of the charges against them, the men began to poke each other and giggle. The authorities refused to believe men this foolish could ever be involved in or plan a massive conspiracy. They were released.

Ned Bennett, one of Denmark's lieutenants, did not wait to be called before the city council. When he heard about William's accusations, Bennett hurried to the mayor's home. He announced that he wanted to clear his name. His bold act impressed the authorities. Bennett assured the group he was not involved in a revolt. He said he doubted such a plot existed. Surely, he said, he would have heard about it if it existed. The white men were satisfied, and Bennett was released.

When Denmark Vesey learned that some of his top conspirators had appeared before Charleston authorities, he became worried that the plot was in jeopardy. Even though the authorities had let the men go, Vesey decided to move up the date of the rebellion before any more details of his plot were leaked. He still hoped that the rebels could catch authorities and slave owners off guard.

Whispers of Conspiracy

Denmark's fears about further leaks were justified. Before long, a slave named George Wilson informed his master that he, too, had been asked to join the rebellion. Wilson said it was to take place on Sunday, June 16, the new date Vesey had settled on. Again, the mayor and governor were informed. This time, instead of dismissing the danger, they notified the captains of the state militia. On the appointed Sunday night, four hundred members of the state militia were assigned to guard the city.

Charleston citizens still had not been told of the plot, but with troops gathering in the city, both black and white citizens knew something was wrong. Whispers that a conspiracy was afoot circulated. A white man named William Hasell Wilson, who was ten years old at the time, later wrote in his memoirs, "I shall never forget the feeling of alarm and anxiety that pervaded the whole community from the time the danger became known, until all the risk appeared to be over." Tensions on Sunday were especially high. "No one, not even the children, ventured to retire," Wilson wrote. "The passing of the patrols on the streets, and every slight noise, excited alarm."[25]

Charleston

British settlers founded the city of Charleston in 1670, and it quickly became an important and wealthy port city. Situated on a peninsula between the Ashley and Cooper rivers, the city exported rice and indigo from nearby plantations. Between 1670 and 1790 the city also served as South Carolina's capital. Initially called Charles Town in honor of King Charles II of England, the city was renamed shortly after the Revolutionary War.

Denmark and Captain Vesey arrived in Charleston around 1783. Vesey leased an office on East Bay Street and lived four blocks away on King Street. Both buildings were near the city's market and wharves. Merchants generally occupied buildings closest to the wharves, but farther from the docks were stately homes. Wide streets covered in a mixture of sand and oyster shells cut paths through the city.

In 1820, just before the Vesey uprising, Charleston was the sixth-largest city in the United States. Over 13,500 slaves and about 1,500 free blacks lived in the area. The white population was about 10,500. The fact that blacks outnumbered whites must have given Denmark Vesey confidence that his plot could succeed.

Though Vesey's plot failed, in 1861 the Civil War broke out in Charleston. Confederate soldiers attacked Union troops at Fort Sumter in the city's harbor. The war ultimately led to freedom for all American slaves.

Boats crowd a harbor in Charleston, South Carolina in the 1760s.

The revolt never occurred. A man Vesey sent to the countryside to signal the start of the uprising never completed his mission. After riding out of town, the messenger found the area heavily patrolled by guardsmen. He knew he would be unable to alert the slaves and returned with the news. Vesey understood. The authorities knew too much. He told his lieutenants to burn their lists of conspirators. He then went into hiding.

On the basis of confessions of would-be rebels, or perhaps black spies sent by Mayor Hamilton, some of Vesey's lieutenants—Peter Poyas, Ned Bennett, and Rolla Bennett—were taken into custody on June 18. Other rebels were also rounded up and sent to the city's workhouse. Four days later, Denmark Vesey was found and arrested. But authorities had yet to uncover the extent of the plot. Confronted with conspirators who refused to talk, authorities used promises of pardons as well as threats to get more information about the plot. Some slaves who would not cooperate were flogged. Eventually, more than 130 people were arrested in connection with the uprising.

Even as the plot began to unravel, many Charleston slave owners had a hard time believing that their slaves wished them harm. Some, thinking their slaves innocent, hired the best attorneys for them when they were brought to trial. Other masters, having heard the evidence against their property, confronted the slaves. One master asked his coachman, who had been arrested, what he had planned to do. The slave owner could hardly have been comforted by the reply: "To kill you, rip open your belly [and] throw your guts in your face." [26]

The Trials

Trials for the accused conspirators lasted five and a half weeks. Perhaps fittingly, it was the Negro Act of 1740, which had been enacted after the Stono Rebellion, that guided the court in punishing the rebels. Day after day, in proceedings that were closed to the public, conspirators were brought before a court that assembled in Charleston's workhouse.

Denmark Vesey's trial began on June 26 and was one of the last. Over the next two days, four slaves testified against him. Even the wigmaker from whom Vesey had bought hairpieces took the stand. During most of the trial, Vesey sat with his arms folded and his eyes fixed on the floor. Dissatisfied with his lawyer, he cross-examined witnesses himself, hoping to trip them up. He also gave an impassioned speech. Why, he asked the court, would a free man be involved in such a plot? Despite such a logical question, so many people accused Denmark Vesey of being the plot's mastermind that he was found guilty.

"You *Ought* to Have Known"

On June 27, 1822, Denmark Vesey was taken from his cell and brought into the courtroom on the upper floor of the workhouse. A judge read his sentence:

> Denmark Vesey: the Court, on mature consideration, have pronounced you guilty. You have enjoyed the advantage of able Counsel, and were also heard in your own [defense], in which you endeavored, with great art and plausibility, to impress a belief of your innocence. After the most patient deliberation, however, the Court were not only satisfied of your guilt, but that you were the author and original instigator of this diabolical plot. Your professed design was to trample on all laws, human and divine; to riot in blood, outrage, rapine, and conflagration, and to introduce anarchy and confusion in their most horrid forms. Your life has become, therefore, a just and necessary sacrifice, at the shrine of indignant justice. It is difficult to imagine what *infatuation* could have prompted you to attempt an enterprise so wild and visionary. You were a free man; were comparatively wealthy; and enjoyed every comfort compatible with your situation. You had, therefore, much to risk, and little to gain. From your age and experience, you *ought* to have known, that success was impracticable.[27]

Vesey was sentenced to hang. As he heard his sentence read, one observer saw a single tear run down Vesey's cheek and heard him whisper that the work of the insurrection would go on. Vesey was one of thirty-five men who would die for their involvement in the plot. Others were sentenced to be whipped or sold away to slave owners in foreign countries.

On July 2, Vesey and five other convicted conspirators were led from their cells at the workhouse. The group included some of Vesey's oldest friends and leading conspirators—Rolla and Ned Bennett and Peter Poyas. None of the men said anything as they climbed into a cart bound for Blake's Lands, a desolate area outside the city. Though it was uncomfortably hot outside, many black and white Charleston residents lined the streets to catch a glimpse of the men. Others gathered at Blake's Lands to witness

The Vesey Family

Denmark Vesey may have been free, but slavery still affected him deeply, especially since close family members were still slaves. Historians do not know all the details of Vesey's family life, but it appears that at the time of the insurrection Denmark had at least three children who were slaves: Sandy, Robert, and Polydore. Because their mother, Beck, was a slave, all her children became slaves. It appears that either Denmark did not have enough money to purchase his children or their owner refused to sell them.

Seeing his children enslaved had a powerful effect on Vesey. It "ate into Vesey's mind," according to Archibald Grimké, one of Denmark Vesey's first biographers. Monday Gell, one of Vesey's lieutenants, testified that Vesey had confided that he "wished to see what could be done for [his children]," meaning that he hoped rebellion would lead to their freedom.

Although Denmark's children were slaves, it seemed he did have a role in their lives. Robert Vesey became a carpenter like his father. Sandy Vesey learned to read and write and was part of the rebellion plot. He was eventually deported for his role in the conspiracy.

After the failed rebellion and Denmark's death, Vesey's children are hard to trace. Polydore's name does not appear again in the public record. City authorities never revealed where slaves such as Sandy were deported. Historians know that at least some men convicted during the rebellion were sent to the Spanish colony of Cuba as slaves. In 1825 three slaves expelled from Charleston for their role in a planned insurrection were arrested for plotting a revolt in Cuba. It is possible that Sandy Vesey was one of these men, following in the footsteps of his father.

Historians know the most about what happened to Robert Vesey. According to one source, the carpenter returned to Charleston after the Civil War. He then became the architect of Charleston's new AME church, replacing the building where his father had recruited lieutenants and the structure that had been razed after the rebellion plot was discovered.

Quoted in Douglas R. Egerton, *He Shall Go Out Free: The Lives of Denmark Vesey.* Madison, WI: Madison House 1999, p. 82.

the executions. But if the spectators expected to see the rebels express remorse, they were disappointed. Mayor Hamilton reported in a letter that the men "met their fate with the heroic fortitude of Martyrs."[28]

The Legacies of Denmark Vesey

Even with Denmark and his co-conspirators dead, the rebels' plot shook South Carolina. Over the next several years, both the city of Charleston and the state of South Carolina took measures to prevent future insurrections. In December 1822, the Charleston City Council created a new group of guards, to number 150, for the city. They patrolled the city's streets around the clock. Any slave found outside without a pass after 9 P.M. could be taken to the guardhouse and flogged. On Sunday mornings, when most Charleston residents attended church services, two patrolmen guarded each church.

Authorities responded in other ways as well. Charleston's City Council announced that it would enforce laws against teaching slaves to read and write. The state legislature placed additional restrictions on slaves who hired out. Finally, Charleston's African Methodist Episcopal church was demolished.

Free blacks were targeted, too. Worried that South Carolina might be harboring other men with Denmark Vesey's intentions, officials created new laws intended to drive free blacks out of the state. One law required any free black man older than fifteen to have a white guardian. Another law mandated that free blacks register with the city twice a year and pay an annual $50 tax, a substantial sum that few blacks could afford. Finally, any free black person who left the state was prohibited from reentering.

Although Vesey's rebellion led to tightened restrictions, his story also became an inspiration to many blacks. As slaves struggled for freedom, black leaders like Frederick Douglass invoked Vesey's name in speeches. Recruiting for a black regiment to fight in the Civil War, Douglass rallied a cheering New York crowd by saying, "Remember Denmark Vesey of Charleston."[29]

Chapter Five

Nat Turner's Rebellion

The best-known slave rebellion in U.S. history began on August 22, 1831. Led by thirty-one-year-old Nat Turner, a group of rebel slaves rampaged through Southampton County in southeastern Virginia. For nearly twenty-four hours they marched and killed unchallenged. The wake of death they left was unparalleled by any slave rebellion the United States had ever seen. Ultimately, although the rebels numbered fewer than seventy, more than fifty white citizens lost their lives.

Nat Turner

Nat Turner was born on October 2, 1800. He was a slave of Benjamin Turner, a farmer who lived in Southampton County, along Virginia's border with North Carolina. The area was rural, 70 or 80 miles (113 or 129km) from big cities like Norfolk and Richmond. Most farmers in the area raised cows, hogs, and chickens and grew corn, cotton, potatoes, and peas. Nat grew up working in the fields.

Not much else is known about Turner's early life. His father escaped from slavery when Nat was a youngster; Nat had several different masters as he was growing up, though he stayed in Southampton County. After Benjamin Turner died, Nat

Nat Turner grew up working in cotton fields such as this one.

became the property of his brother Samuel and was later sold to Thomas Moore. Then Moore died, leaving Nat to his nine-year-old son Putnam. When Putnam's mother remarried, Turner's new master was Joseph Travis.

One constant in Nat Turner's life, however, was his faith. Turner's grandmother was extremely religious, and he studied the Bible from a very young age. Family and friends also noticed that as a child Nat seemed to remember events that had happened before his birth. Because of this, they believed that the youth had special powers.

The Spirit Speaks

At some point in his youth, Turner began to experience visions. These further confirmed the suspicions of friends and relatives that he was possessed of special gifts. Those visions set Turner on a fateful path. A series of nine revelations spread out over several years eventually convinced Turner that it was his destiny to lead a rebellion.

Still, the earliest revelations Turner experienced said nothing of revolution. Turner was praying at his plow in the field when the first vision came upon him. Remembering the event years later, he recalled, "The spirit spoke to me, saying 'Seek ye the kingdom of Heaven and all things shall be added unto you.'"[30] For the next two years, Turner prayed regularly. A second and third revelation persuaded him to speak to others in earnest about the messages of these revelations.

Sometime after his twenty-second birthday, Turner was placed under a new overseer who historians believe was harsher than his predecessor had been. In reaction to the stricter regime, Turner ran away, hiding in the woods for a month. But the spirit, he said, convinced him to return, to the surprise and anger of many fellow slaves. Another revelation came to him shortly after he returned. In it Turner saw the sun darken and black and white spirits engage in battle.

In the spring of 1828, Turner's revelations began to lead him to revolution. Again, while working in the fields, Turner experienced a vision in which a spirit told him to "fight against the Serpent."[31] Turner concluded that the "Serpent" was a reference to slave owners and took the spirit's words to mean that he should plot a rebellion. He began waiting for a sign that the time had come to begin his uprising.

It took almost three years, but when Turner saw a solar eclipse on February 12, 1831, he believed it was his sign. Taking several other slaves into his confidence, Turner planned an uprising for July 4, 1831, Independence Day. But Turner fell ill, and the plot had to be postponed.

Later that summer, on a day in August, the sun rose with what Turner later said was an odd green tint that later turned to blue. In the afternoon a dark spot appeared on the sun's surface. Believing this strange sight was a second sign, Turner gathered six confidants on the night of Sunday, August 21. Historians cannot be sure how well planned the rebellion was or what exactly Turner wanted to accomplish with his plot, but shortly after midnight Turner began an uprising that would stun slave owners.

The Rebellion Begins

Turner slipped into Joseph Travis's house through a second-story window. The family had just returned from evening church services and had settled into their beds. As they slept, Turner unbarred the home's door and let in the other rebels. Armed with a hatchet, an ax, and some guns from the house, the men tiptoed into Travis's bedroom. Turner struck the first blow, swinging a hatchet toward his master's head. The man woke up screaming before a second rebel killed him with a blow from an ax. Four more family members, including an infant, were killed as they slept. The insurrection had begun.

Under the cover of darkness, the rebels took more firearms and ammunition from the home. They practiced several drills in the family's barn and then marched to the nearby farmhouse of Salathul Francis, where they knocked on the door. Francis, the only white occupant, answered. The rebels grabbed him and dragged him outside, killing him with blows to the head. Then they moved on, entering through an unlocked door the home of Piety Reese and murdering her and her son in their beds.

By this time day was breaking. The news that a rebellion was under way was slow to spread among local whites. As a result, the rebels were able to approach and shoot some people outdoors— one as he stood in a cotton patch, another group as they worked at a still. The rebels also brazenly chopped down doors with axes and chased down the men and women they found inside. No one was spared the group's wrath. Turner later related what happened to one woman who tried to escape: "Mrs. Williams fled and got some distance from the house, but she was pursued, overtaken, and compelled to get up behind one of the company, who

Turner (center) discusses his plan with co-conspirators.

brought her back, and after showing her the mangled body of her lifeless husband, she was told to get down and lay by his side, where she was shot dead."[32]

By the afternoon of August 22, the rebels had marched over 20 miles (32km), cutting a swath of death and destruction. At least fifty-seven white men, women, and children were dead. Meanwhile, the rebels had gathered recruits and arms as they moved.

A Confrontation

With much bloody work behind them, Turner's rebels marched toward the town of Jerusalem, the county seat and the location of a considerable cache of arms. On the way the men stopped at the home of James W. Parker. Though Parker was away, some of the rebels had family members working at the Parker place and wanted to recruit them to the insurrection. Turner agreed to stop, but the stop would be the rebels' last.

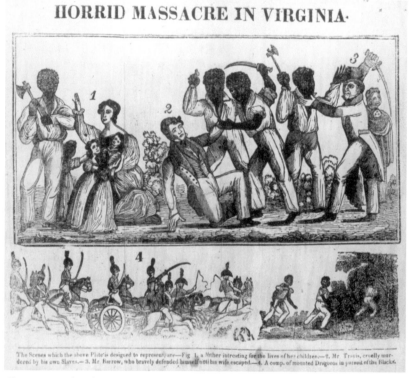

HORRID MASSACRE IN VIRGINIA·

The Scenes which the above Plate is designed to represent are—Fig 1, a Mother intreating for the lives of her children.—2, Mr Travis, cruelly murdered by his own Slaves.—3, Mr. Barrow, who bravely defended himself until his wife escaped.—4, A comp. of mounted Dragoons in pursuit of the Blacks.

Slaves attack whites in this 1831 depiction of Nat Turner's rebellion. Almost sixty people were killed in the uprising.

While the rebels waited, eighteen white men approached, guns firing. Following the bloodstained track, the whites had finally caught up with the rebels. Surprised by the attack, Turner struggled to rally his men. The rebels managed to drive their attackers back, but the victory was short-lived.

When Turner's rebels advanced against their attackers again, they found that a second party of whites had met up with the first. All the men were loading their guns. Meanwhile, several of Turner's most capable men had been wounded in the fighting. Others had panicked and fled. Resupplied with ammunition, the white men charged again. This time, most of the rebels scattered. Turner remembered:

The white men pursued and fired on us several times. [One of my men] had his horse shot under him, and I caught another for him as it was running by me; five or six of my men were wounded, but none left on the field: finding myself defeated here I instantly determined to go through a private way . . . accompanied by about twenty men, I overtook two or three who told me others were dispersed in every direction.[33]

At first, Turner hoped that his force could regroup. He believed that if they could get to Jerusalem by a different route, they would be able to attack the city and obtain more weapons and ammunition to continue their rebellion. But Turner could not muster

---

A Slave Remembers Turner's Rebellion

Henry "Box" Brown was about fifteen years old and working on a Virginia tobacco farm during the time of the Turner rebellion. His master told him very little about the insurrection, only that some slaves had tried to kill their masters. Still, Brown saw panic sweep the area and remembered the violent backlash against slaves.

In the late 1840s, almost two decades after Turner's rebellion, Brown dramatically escaped Virginia and slavery by mailing himself to Philadelphia. He had a local carpenter build a box—3 feet long by 2 feet wide by about 2.5 feet tall (0.9m by 0.6m by 0.76m)—and nail him inside for the twenty-four-hour journey. Brown's escape made him famous, and he published his life story in 1849. He described the aftermath of Turner's rebellion this way:

> I have since learned that it was the famous Nat Turner's insurrection that caused all the excitement I witnessed. Slaves were whipped, hung, and cut down with swords in the streets, if found away from their quarters after dark. The whole city was in the utmost confusion and dismay. . . . Great numbers of the slaves were locked in the prison, and many were "half hung," as it was termed; that is, they were suspended [from] some limb of a tree, with a rope about their necks so adjusted as not to quite strangle them, and then they were pelted by the men and boys with rotten eggs. This half-hanging is a refined species of cruelty, peculiar to slavery, I believe.

Quoted in Eric Foner, ed., *Great Lives Observed: Nat Turner.* Englewood Cliffs, NJ: Prentice Hall, 1971, pp. 67–68.

enough men to march on Jerusalem. He recounted, "After [trying] in vain to collect a sufficient force to proceed to Jerusalem, I determined to return, as I was sure they would make back to their old neighborhood, where they would rejoin me, make new recruits, and come down again."[34] In fact, Turner's rebel band never regained its strength. That evening, Turner attempted to recruit more slaves, but when the group arrived at the home of a white man known as Captain Harris, a group of armed whites confronted Turner's band again. The rebels quickly fled.

Hunting Nat Turner

Pursued and alone, Turner abandoned his plot and went into hiding. The entire state of Virginia, meanwhile, was in an uproar. Flyers announcing a reward for Turner's capture were tacked to doors and tree trunks. Newspapers ran reward announcements. But no one had seen the rebel leader. Some newspapers erroneously reported that Turner had escaped to Maryland or to the West Indies. There were reports he had been taken prisoner in Washington, D.C.; other accounts said that he had drowned.

In fact, Turner never left the area where the rebellion took place. He later explained, "On Thursday night after having supplied myself with provisions . . . I scratched a hole under a pile of fence rails in the field, where I concealed myself . . . never leaving my hiding place but for a few minutes in the dead of night to get water which was very near."[35]

After six weeks of concealment, Turner became bolder, venturing out of his hiding spot for longer periods of time. Some nights he would stand outside houses, eavesdropping on conversations in hopes of learning what authorities were doing. He spoke to no one, kept himself carefully concealed, and always returned to his hiding place before dawn.

Despite his care, one night a dog roving the neighborhood smelled a piece of meat Turner had stored in his hideaway and stole it. A few nights later, the dog was out hunting with two slaves. Returning to the spot where he had found the meat, the dog discovered Turner and began barking. His hiding place revealed, Turner confessed to being the rebel leader, and the two surprised slaves fled. Turner knew they would notify the authorities, so he found himself a new hiding place.

Nat Turner surrenders to Benjamin Phipps after slaves found him hiding near the site of the rebellion.

After he was seen, however, everyone in Southampton County was on the alert. Eager citizens combed the countryside, hoping to catch the rebel leader and collect the advertised rewards. On October 30, 1831, Benjamin Phipps, a white farmer, found Turner, armed only with an old sword, hiding in a hole under a fallen tree. The hunt for the rebel leader was over. Newspapers throughout the South soon proclaimed "The Bandit Taken" and "Nat Turner Surely Is Captured."[36]

Jailhouse Confession

Locked up in the Southampton County jail, Turner knew what was in store for him. Many whites wanted not only justice but revenge. More than forty of his men had already been tried. Many had been hanged. Some had been decapitated and their heads impaled on poles along the road. Turner had led the rebellion. He could expect no mercy.

Still, while Turner had been in hiding, many questions about the rebellion surfaced. Accounts of the event had been exaggerated and twisted. Citizens wanted to know who Turner was and why he had led the uprising. A local lawyer, Thomas Ruffin Gray, visited the jail to talk with Turner and find out the answers.

Gray had already represented some of the other men accused of being part of the plot. He had also ridden with a party of volunteers pursuing the rebels and later traced the entire rebel route, viewing the bloody crime scenes. As a result, Gray knew a lot about the rebellion. Over several days, Gray questioned Turner in his jail cell and listened to him tell his story. Later, he produced a pamphlet with Turner's first-person account called *The Confessions of Nat Turner*. In it, Turner described the insurrection in

Wanted: Nat Turner

After the insurrection, many newspapers published a proclamation from Virginia governor John Floyd offering a $500 reward for Nat Turner's capture. It included a description of him so that people would know what he looked like. It read:

> Nat is between 30 & 35 [years old], 5 feet 6 or 8 inches high, weighs between 150 and 160 pounds, rather bright complexion, but not a mulatto, broad shouldered, large flat nose, large eyes, broad flat feet, rather [knock-kneed], walks brisk and active, hair on the top of the head very thin, no beard, except on the upper lip and the top of the chin, a scar on one of his temples, also one on the back of his neck, a large knot on one of the bones of his right arm, near the wrist, produced by a blow.

Quoted in Henry I. Tragle, *The Southampton Slave Revolt of 1831: A Compilation of Source Material.* Amherst: The University of Massachusetts Press, 1971, p. 421.

meticulous and sometimes grisly detail and Gray recounted part of Turner's trial. When the pamphlet was published, citizens quickly snapped up all forty thousand copies, in hopes of understanding what made the slave rebel.

Not a Shadow of Doubt

On November 5, 1831, Nat Turner was called before the court in Jerusalem, Virginia. The court of oyer and terminer in which he was tried provided him with a lawyer, William C. Parker, who was paid $10 for defending the rebel leader.

The trial itself was short. Turner pleaded not guilty. One witness for the prosecution testified that he had seen several of the rebels murder members of his family. Nat Turner, he said, was in charge of the group. Parker did not call any witnesses or introduce evidence on the rebel leader's behalf. In all likelihood it would not have mattered if he had. The justices were convinced from the outset that Turner was guilty. At some point, the judges heard a version of Thomas Gray's *Confessions*, which was read in Nat Turner's presence and which he acknowledged was true. That dispelled any doubts they might have had. According to Gray's account of the trial in the *Confessions*, the last exchange between Turner and a judge went this way:

> Jeremiah Cobb: "Nat Turner! Stand up. Have you anything to say why sentence of death should not be pronounced against you?"
>
> Nat: "I have not. I have made a full confession to Mr. Gray, and I have nothing more to say."
>
> Cobb: "Attend then to the sentence of the Court. You have been arraigned and tried before this court, and convicted of one of the highest crimes in our criminal code. You have been convicted of plotting in cold blood, the indiscriminate destruction of men, of helpless women, and of infant children. The evidence before us leaves not a shadow of doubt, but that your hands were often imbrued in the blood of the innocent; and your own confession tells us that they were stained with the blood of a master." [37]

Cobb continued, "The judgment of the court is, that you be taken hence to the jail from whence you came, thence to the place of execution, and on Friday next, between the hours of 10 A.M. and 2 P.M. be hung by the neck until you are dead! dead! dead! And may the Lord have mercy upon your soul."[38]

Some fifty blacks would eventually stand trial for their roles in the plot. Nineteen would hang.

On November 11, at about one o'clock, Turner was led to the hanging tree in Jerusalem. A large crowd had assembled, and Turner was asked if he had any final words. He did not. But the rebel leader had one more surprise in store for spectators at his hanging. The newspaper *The Liberator* reported that "not a limb nor a muscle was observed to move"[39] as he died. Perhaps as a final act of resistance, Turner refused to give the crowd the satisfaction of seeing him struggle.

Panic in Virginia

Even as Turner was being led to his death, his rebellion continued to created panic. News of the uprising created a backlash against blacks. One historian estimates that at least 120 blacks—and probably many more—were killed by angry whites in the wake of the rebellion. Whatever the number, it was likely far more than the number of whites murdered by the rebels and more than the number of blacks who participated in the rebellion.

Even as the initial backlash subsided, many Virginians remained on edge. One woman described her unease at the possibility of another rebellion. "It is like a smothered volcano," she wrote: "we know not when, or where, the flame will burst forth but we know that death in the most horrid forms threaten us. Some have died, others have become deranged from apprehension since the [Nat Turner] affair."[40] A man from Virginia explained that he feared noises in the night: "A corn song, or a hog call, has often been the subject of nervous terror, and a cat, in the dining room, will banish sleep for the night."[41]

Turner's Legacy

While the Turner rebellion prompted immediate widespread fear and suspicion among whites, it had longer-term consequences,

Angry whites set a black man on fire after he is hanged. Turner was hanged in 1831 after being found guilty of leading a slave rebellion.

too. After the uprising many states, including North Carolina, Alabama, Maryland, and Virginia, rushed to restrict the activities of blacks, both slave and free. In Maryland, free blacks were barred from immigrating to the state, and free blacks already in the state were not allowed to own weapons. A new law restricted all blacks from holding religious services without whites present. Whites were forbidden to sell liquor to blacks.

In Virginia, where the rebellion took place, the uprising resulted in new laws, too. As in Maryland, a new law banned slaves and free blacks from holding religious services or meetings of their own. Laws also outlawed the sale of liquor to slaves. In addition, free blacks saw their right to a trial by jury eliminated.

The Virginia Slavery Debates

One of the most important consequences of Nat Turner's rebellion, however, was the debate over slavery it prompted in the Virginia legislature. Some Virginians believed that the uprising

No Tombstone for Nat Turner

On November 14, 1831, *The Norfolk Herald* reported that before he died, "Nat sold his body for dissection, and spent the money in ginger cakes." Historians agree that this report is certainly false and simply another attempt to discredit the rebel leader. But what did happen to Nat Turner's body? That is a mystery that has always intrigued historians.

William S. Drewry, a historian at the turn of the twentieth century, was one of the first people to investigate seriously what happened to Turner's body. After conducting his own interviews, Drewry believed that "Nat Turner's body was delivered to the doctors, who skinned it and made grease of the flesh." Drewry reported that a doctor had owned Turner's skeleton for many years, but it had been misplaced.

Not everyone agreed with Drewry's analysis. Virginia resident Frances Lawrence Webb wrote in her memoir that Turner's headless body was buried near where he was hanged. A local physician was given his skull and later passed it on to a northern university, she said. Webb's story may have merit. In August 1902 an Ohio newspaper reported that Nat Turner's skull had survived a fire at the College of Wooster, and novelist William Styron, who published a book about the Turner rebellion in 1967, received a letter from a man who said he had seen Turner's skull at the college repeatedly as a child.

Whether or not the skull at the College of Wooster was Turner's, it is certainly possible that it was one of the Turner rebels. Contemporary reports say that militia units cut off several rebels' heads during the rebellion, and other reports say that whites carried the heads around as trophies. Any one of these heads might have later been labeled as Turner's.

Norfolk Herald, November 14, 1831, in *The Confessions of Nat Turner and Related Documents*, ed. Kenneth S. Greenberg. Boston: Bedford/St. Martin's, 1996, p. 90.

Quoted in Kenneth S. Greenberg. ed., *The Confessions of Nat Turner and Related Documents*. Boston: Bedford/St. Martin's, 1996, p. 19.

should be taken as a call to abolish slavery. Virginia governor John Floyd, for example, confided in his diary that he hoped to see Virginia pass a law that would gradually outlaw slavery in the state.

When Virginia's legislative session opened in December, three weeks after Turner's execution, a petition to abolish slavery was introduced. In January 1832, Thomas Jefferson Randolph, grandson of the late president Thomas Jefferson, proposed a referendum on ending slavery in Virginia.

Under Randolph's proposal, all slaves born on or after July 4, 1840, would become the property of the state when they reached a certain age—men when they turned twenty-one and women when they turned eighteen. Slaves could still be sold to owners in another state before this time. Otherwise, they would be transported from the state. The planned abolition was gradual, but it would leave about where the state's leaders stood, no doubts. If such a law were enacted, Virginia would eventually have no slaves, and Nat Turner's rebellion would have been the catalyst for a major change.

For the next two months, legislators argued over the merits of slavery and colonization—that is resettling former slaves in Africa. The debate was unprecedented in the South. The Richmond *Whig* declared, "Nat Turner, and the blood of his innocent victims, have conquered the silence of fifty years."[42] Yet many southern whites were shocked. They worried that the debates might motivate even more slaves to rebel.

The Virginia legislature, however, never did pass an emancipation statute. Ultimately, all the legislature could agree on was that colonization was too complicated and costly to work. The 1832 debates were the last time that the possibility of emancipation was openly debated in the South. It would take more than three decades and a bloody civil war before Virginia's slaves—and those in other states—were free and Nat Turner's vision realized.

Chapter Six

The *Amistad* Rebellion

In the early morning hours of July 2, 1839, the long, low schooner *Amistad* lay anchored off the coast of Cuba, a few days' sail from its destination, Cuba's Puerto Principe. The ship's timbers creaked, and water lapped at its sides. On deck, the ship's captain and cook slept soundly. In their cabins below, two slave owners had also gone to bed. Chained below decks, however, forty-nine African men and four children were wide awake and plotting rebellion.

The Africans were slaves, recently taken from their homes and sent in chains across the Atlantic Ocean to Cuba. There they had been sold at a Havana slave market. The rebellion they were plotting would begin a journey that would take them to the United States. For the next two years, they would have to fight in court for the right to return home. Ultimately, against all odds, the rebellious slaves would gain their freedom.

Slavery Bound

The fifty-three captives aboard the *Amistad* had all been enslaved in Africa. Many had been kidnapped. Soldiers took others during wars, and some had been enslaved because they had committed a crime. After being sold to slave traders and spending more than two months at sea, the Africans were brought to a slave market in Havana. Though importing slaves into Cuba was a violation of Spanish law, slavery itself was legal on the island and slave trading very profitable. Slave traders who managed to land in Cuba without getting caught easily found buyers for their African cargo while officials looked the other way.

In Havana's slave market, the captives were quickly purchased by two Spaniards, José Ruiz and Pedro Montes. Ruiz was only twenty-four years old, but he was already a successful business-man. He purchased forty-nine men for $450 each and planned to transport them to Puerto Principe. There, he hoped to resell the men to plantation owners at a profit. Montes, meanwhile, pur-chased the four children, three girls and a boy, perhaps to keep as slaves in his own home.

To transport their slave cargo and other items they planned to sell, the two men chartered the schooner *Amistad*. The ship's captain, Ramón Ferrer, would sail the schooner along with two white crew members and help from two of his own slaves. Though the slaves in the hold vastly outnumbered the crew, the slave owners did not expect any trouble. The slaves had other plans.

Rebellion

One of the captives, named Cinqué, was determined to regain his freedom. When night fell and he and the other captives were chained in the hold, he produced a nail he had found on deck while unchained for exercise. With it, he picked the locks secur-ing him and his companions. Freed, several of the men stole into the ship's cargo area. They discovered that the ship was trans-porting luxury items and plantation supplies, including large knives for cutting sugarcane. While some of the men stayed behind with the children, the rest armed themselves with the knives and crept on deck.

Shouting and swinging their weapons, the slaves surprised the sleeping captain and cook. The slave owners, Ruiz and Montes, awoke to hear screams and thumps. They rushed to the deck. The captain and cook were already dead, lying in pools of blood, and the two white crew members had disappeared, possibly hav-ing jumped overboard in an attempt to swim to shore. The slave

owners and the black cabin boy all surrendered. The slaves had control of the ship, but they were far from home and freedom.

In fact, the Africans had no idea how to steer the ship. Cinqué, who had been allowed up on deck at some point during the voyage from Africa, understood that to return, the boat needed to head into the sun during the day, sailing east. But he did not know how the sails worked or how to keep the ship on course at night. Using signs and gestures to communicate, Cinqué ordered Montes and Ruiz to help sail the ship back to Africa, and they agreed.

The Spaniards, however, had no intention of honoring their pledge. They believed they had a better chance of getting their slaves back if the schooner stayed near Cuba or sailed north to the United States. They hoped that the *Amistad* would be picked up by another ship or land in territory where slavery was legal. The fact that the Africans knew nothing about using stars to navigate worked to the Spaniards' advantage. Ruiz and Montes deceived the slaves, allowing the ship to head east toward Africa by day, but then turning it west at night. Montes later explained, "I steered for Havana, in the night by the stars, but by the sun in the day, taking care to make no more way than possible."[43]

An illustration from 1840 depicts the slave uprising that killed Captain Ramón Ferrer on board the *Amistad.*

The Wandering Ship

As a result of this deception, for the next two months the ship took on a zigzag course. Eventually, those on board ran out of food and freshwater. In desperation, some of the Africans drank full bottles of medicine they found in the ship's hold and died. In total, ten Africans died from starvation, illness, or wounds they had received during the uprising. Finally, on August 26, 1839, the *Amistad* anchored off New York's Long Island. A group of Africans took a rowboat and went ashore to look for food. Meanwhile, a U.S. Navy ship, the USS *Washington*, sailed into view. Sailors aboard the *Washington* grew suspicious of the schooner. The *Amistad* flew no flag to identify where it had come from. Its sails were hanging in tatters, and as the *Washington* approached, sailors could see that barnacles were growing on the ship's hull, a sign of disrepair. Stranger still was the group on deck—black men wearing little or no clothing and with no white men in sight. The *Washington* sailors decided to board the *Amistad.*

Seeing the *Washington* approach, the Africans on shore scrambled back into their rowboat. Although they rowed furiously, the *Washington's* sailors got to the *Amistad* first. They quickly boarded and took control of the ship. It seemed that the Africans' hopes

A reconstruction of the *Amistad* sails in a Connecticut seaport. After the rebellion, the original *Amistad* was towed to New London, Connecticut.

of returning home were dashed. Meanwhile, Ruiz and Montes were overjoyed. The slave owners fell on their knees, weeping and thanking the sailors for rescuing them. Then they told their story to the ship's officers, Lieutenant Richard W. Meade and the ship's commander Lieutenant Thomas R. Gedney, who decided to take the ship to a port and report their findings to the authorities.

A Judge and Jail for the Africans

With the *Amistad* in tow, the *Washington* sailed for the nearby port of New London, Connecticut. There, the officers turned the case over to a judge, Andrew T. Judson. The judge listened to the slave owners' story of the rebellion and inspected the ship. Judson decided that the circuit court meeting in Hartford, Connecticut, in September would need to hear the case. There, a judge would

Cinqué led the *Amistad* rebellion. Upon reaching America, he and his fellow slaves were jailed.

decide whether the slaves should stand trial for mutiny and murder as a result of their rebellion.

Until their court date, the *Amistad* captives were jailed nearby in New Haven. Ruiz and Montes were free. Newspapers picked up the story of the strange ship, and curious visitors arrived in New Haven in droves. Blacks had lived in the state for generations, but Africans were a novel sight for Connecticut residents. Moreover, almost all Connecticut blacks were free, the result of the state's 1784 gradual emancipation act. By the time of the *Amistad* rebels' first trial, some four thousand people had visited the jail—and paid twelve and a half cents admission to see the prisoners.

The *Amistad* Rebels Find Friends

Among the visitors were students and professors from nearby Yale University. They visited daily and tried to communicate with the Africans and to teach them English. Dr. Josiah Willard Gibbs, a linguistics professor, was a regular visitor. By patiently holding up his fingers one by one and prompting the Africans to count, Gibbs learned the numbers one through ten in the Africans' language. Gibbs then traveled to New York and combed the city's docks, where many blacks worked. Gibbs counted to every black person he saw, "Eta, fili, kiau-wa . . ." one, two, three—in the hopes of finding someone who recognized the language. Finally, Gibbs met James Covey, a former slave who had been captured in Sierra Leone. Covey had spoken the Africans' language, which he said was called Mende, as a child. Through Covey, the Africans were finally able to tell their side of the rebellion story. With a translator at their side, the Africans would at least be able to argue in court for their freedom.

There was more good news to come. In New York, a group had formed to aid the captives. Headed by abolitionist Lewis Tappan, the group called itself the Committee for the Defense of the Africans of the *Amistad* or, more simply, the *Amistad* Committee. The group began collecting money for the captives and looking after their welfare, buying them clothing and, more important, building a fund to pay for their defense. As the Africans' trial date approached, the committee also chose lawyers for the group. To head the defense, the committee picked New Haven attorney

Roger Baldwin. They also chose Seth Staples, an able lawyer who would later found Yale Law School, and Theodore Sedgwick, a prominent New York attorney.

But opponents of freedom for the Africans began organizing, too. Among those who claimed that the Africans should remain slaves was the Spanish government, which pressed U.S. president Martin Van Buren to send the captives back to Cuba. Treaties between the two countries required this, the Spanish said. But

Lewis Tappan

■

Lewis Tappan was the tireless organizer behind the *Amistad* Committee, the abolitionist group that formed to aid the Africans. Even before the Africans landed in the United States, however, Tappan was a well-known and influential abolitionist.

Along with his older brother Arthur, Lewis Tappan had helped found the New York chapter of the American Antislavery Society. The brothers, who were wealthy merchants, gave generously to religious and abolitionist causes.

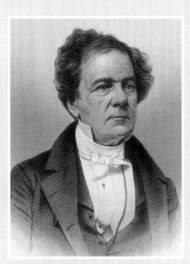

Abolitionist Lewis Tappan organized aid for the *Amistad* Africans.

When Lewis Tappan read about the *Amistad* case in the newspaper in the summer of 1839, he called a meeting of leading abolitionists in New York. For the next two years, Tappan and other abolitionists worked determinedly to raise money, find legal counsel, and help the Africans however they could. Tappan himself was present at the Africans' trials and wrote countless letters to friends and acquaintances on their behalf.

Tappan continued his efforts as an abolitionist after the *Amistad* trial. In 1846 he helped found the American Missionary Association, which sponsored the teaching of antislavery ideas both in the United States and in foreign countries. He died on June 21, 1873.

Van Buren could do little because the case was already in court. He could not usurp the court's authority. Instead, U.S. district attorney W.S. Holabird would appear in court for the government. Holabird was to argue that the state of Connecticut had no business trying the Africans and that they should be turned over to the Spanish government and returned to Cuba. Spanish officials would then determine whether a trial was necessary.

The First Trial

On September 19, 1839, the *Amistad* case opened in the State House in downtown Hartford. City streets were crowded with spectators. Hotels were packed. There were rumors that there was going to be a mass hanging of the captives.

Black Communities and the *Amistad*

Books on the *Amistad* trial often focus on the white abolitionists who worked to free the Africans. It is true that these white abolitionists were crucial in aiding the Africans, but black abolitionists and black citizens also took a great interest in the case. Black groups raised money for the Africans, celebrated the outcome of the trial, and were intimately involved with their return to Africa.

Beginning just weeks after the *Amistad* men were brought ashore in the United States, two black self-improvement societies in New York organized a benefit concert for the group. The $84.08 that the concert raised was reported in the *Colored American*, then the country's only black-run newspaper. *Colored American* publisher Charles Ray continued to update his readers on the *Amistad* case for the next two years. He ultimately published more than eighty articles on the case in his four-page weekly.

A black Philadelphia sailmaker named Robert Purvis also befriended the Africans. Purvis organized donations for the group and met with the Africans personally. He also commissioned a portrait of Cinqué. When the work was completed, he had black and white engravings of it made. Purvis donated the copies to an antislavery society, which sold them for a dollar apiece.

Inside the courtroom, circuit court judge Smith Thompson tried to keep order. Still, the trial began dramatically. The defense team began by asking Judge Thompson for a legal document called a writ of habeas corpus for the three young girls in the group. The writ would force the prosecution to present evidence that the girls had done something wrong. If the prosecution had no such evidence, the girls would go free. But if the judge granted the writ, it would mean more than possible freedom for the girls. He would be admitting that the children and perhaps the entire group had the same rights that whites had in court.

District Attorney Holabird stood up to protest. A writ of habeas corpus could be issued only for people, he shot back. The slaves, he argued, were property. Defense attorney Baldwin had clearly been expecting Holabird's challenge. He called for a marshal to bring the three girls into the courtroom. As the man led the children into the room, they sobbed and clung to him. Baldwin pointed to the children and asked dramatically, were they really nothing more than property?

The trial continued for two more days. Then, on the third day, Holabird stunned the courtroom by reversing his position. He said that no writ was necessary, that the prisoners were not slaves but free people, and that they should be returned to Africa. Apparently, the White House, noticing growing public sympathy for the captives, had decided to minimize any political damage by getting them out of the country. Judge Thompson was not amused at Holabird's change of position. He ordered all remaining arguments to be presented in writing.

On Monday morning, September 23, Thompson announced his decision to a packed courtroom. He denied the defense's motion for a writ of habeas corpus. But he said that the circuit court could not determine whether the Spanish had a right to the Africans as property. That question, he declared, would have to be decided by a second court, the district court.

Back to Court

Judge Andrew T. Judson, who had presided over the initial investigation of the *Amistad*, opened the district court case in the very same room following Thompson's decision. After hearing arguments, Judson would decide whether the *Amistad* captives were property. If so, they would be returned to Ruiz and Montes as slaves. If not, they would go free.

The case would not be a short one. Several delays meant that preliminary issues were argued off and on between October 1839 and January 1840. The second *Amistad* trial finally reopened on January 7, 1840—this time back in New Haven. At nearby Yale University, law students were given the day off to attend the trial. Teachers, students, New Haven citizens, and onlookers filled the courthouse. The trial lasted five days, and testimony sometimes went on for ten hours.

Both the prosecution and the defense put on their best witnesses. Several of the Africans, including Cinqué, testified with James Covey's help as translator. At one point, Cinqué sat on the courtroom floor, holding his hands and feet together to show how he had been chained for the voyage. Both sides also argued over the treaties between Spain and the United States and what U.S. law required the American government to do with the Africans.

Intrigue in New Haven Harbor

While the court proceedings unfolded in full view of the public, shadier maneuverings were going on in New Haven harbor. Unbeknownst to most of the trial's spectators, the U.S. Navy ship *Grampus* had sailed into New Haven harbor at the trial's opening. It was under top secret orders from President Van Buren, who was under increasing pressure from Spain's government. Van Buren had no authority to overrule the courts, but if Judson ruled that the Africans were property, the president intended that they should immediately be sent back to Cuba and their owners. The abolitionists, meanwhile, readied a boat of their own. Should Judson decide against the Africans, the abolitionists planned to kidnap the captives and sail them to freedom in Canada.

On Monday morning, January 13, 1840, Judson read his decision. Stunning the government, Judson ruled that the slave owners had no right to the Africans, who clearly had been recently imported from Africa in violation of the laws of Spain. "Cinqué and [the other captives] shall not sigh for Africa in vain," Judson announced. "Bloody as may be their hands, they shall yet embrace their kindred." [44]

The Final Appeal

Judson had declared the Africans free, but there was little time to celebrate. The government appealed the case to the Supreme Court, the United States' highest judicial body. Abolitionists knew they would need help if they hoped to win again before this court: Five of the Supreme Court's nine justices, including Chief Justice Roger Taney, were Southerners. Abolitionists feared that the Court would be sympathetic to the slave owners and predisposed to turn the Africans over to them.

To help with the case, the abolitionists turned to former president John Quincy Adams. At seventy-three years old, Adams was an elder statesman in American politics and a powerful ally. In addition to serving as the country's sixth

Former U.S. president John Quincy Adams spoke on behalf of the *Amistad* defendants.

president, he had been a senator, U.S. ambassador to several European countries, and President Monroe's secretary of state. At the time of the *Amistad* trial, he was a member of the House of Representatives. More important, Adams had been watching the trials from afar and was familiar with the issue. He agreed to help argue the case.

On February 20, 1841, the *Amistad* case came before the Supreme Court in Washington, D.C. For more than a week, lawyers presented their arguments before the high court. The highlight of the arguments, however, was John Quincy Adams's speech. Everyone was eager to hear him argue on behalf of the Africans. Adams recorded in his diary what speaking before the court was like: "I had been deeply distressed and agitated till the moment when I rose, and then my spirit did not sink within me. . . . I spoke four hours and a half with sufficient method and order to witness little flagging of attention by the judges or the auditory."[45] Adams spoke for another four hours on a second day, going over the requirements of treaties and the actions of the government in the case. Adams's speech was convincing, but his presence was equally important. The distinguished and well-respected statesman was clearly on the Africans' side.

On March 9 the justices announced that they were ready to rule on the case. Adams waited nervously in the courtroom while Justice Joseph Story read the court's decision. The treaties that the two sides had argued over did not apply and the captives did not have to be returned to Cuba, Story said. Furthermore, he said, all human beings have a right to fight for their freedom. The *Amistad* rebels were free.

Rushing out of the courtroom, Adams dashed off letters to Lewis Tappan and Roger Baldwin, who could not be present. "Dear Sir," he wrote to Baldwin. "The decision of The Supreme Court in the case of the Amistad has this moment been delivered by Judge Story. The Captives are free. . . . Yours in great haste and great joy. J.Q. Adams."[46]

Outrage and Celebration

While southerners, Spaniards, and members of Van Buren's administration condemned the justices' ruling, abolitionists, especially the *Amistad* Committee, celebrated. Roger Baldwin wrote back to Adams that the decision was "glorious not only as a triumph of humanity and justice, but as a vindication of our national character from reproach and dishonor."[47] A correspondent for the *Colored American*, at that time the only newspaper in the country run by blacks, wrote, "Justice is satisfied, and the *captives* are free!"[48]

One group was still unaware of the Supreme Court's decision— the *Amistad* captives themselves, who were staying in Connecticut. The Africans knew that the high court would soon rule on their case, and for days before the verdict they were anxious, asking if any news had been received. Then an official arrived carrying a copy of the newspaper. Kale, one of the African children who

Kale's Letter

One of the youngest *Amistad* captives was an eleven-year-old boy named Kale. Kale learned English quickly, and the group's leader, Cinqué, often relied on him to read documents in English to the group.

Just before the Supreme Court trial, Kale wrote a letter to John Quincy Adams. Adams had visited the group, and Kale knew he was working on their case. Even though his English was halting, Kale got his message across powerfully. "All we want is make us free," he told Adams. Kale's letter was reproduced in several newspapers, including the *Emancipator* and the American Anti-Slavery Society's newsletter, the *American and Foreign Anti-Slavery Reporter*. His letter read:

Dear Friend Mr. Adams:

I want to write a letter to you because you love Mende people, and you talk to the grand court. . . .

We want you to ask the Court what we have done wrong. What for Americans keep us in prison? Some people say Mende people crazy; Mende people dolt because we no talk America language. Merica people no talk Mende language; Merica people dolt? . . .

Dear friend Mr. Adams, you have children, you have friends, you love them, you feel very sorry if Mende people come and carry them to Africa. We feel bad for our friends and our friends all feel bad for us. . . . If American people give us free we glad, if they no give us free we sorry—we sorry for Mende people little, we sorry for American people great deal, because God punish liars. We want you to tell court that [we] no want to go back to Havana; we no want to be killed. Dear Friend, we want you to know how we feel. . . . All we want is make us free.

Kale to John Quincy Adams, January 4, 1841. Printed in the *Hartford Daily Courant*. http://amistad.mysticseaport.org/library/letters/mhs.kale.to.jqa.html.

Black Communities React to the Case's Outcome

■

Black churches, abolitionist groups, and the *Colored American* cheered the outcome of the Supreme Court trial. Some black groups held parties celebrating the trial's outcome. Blacks also flocked to see the men on their speaking tours. Some meetings for specifically black audiences drew larger and more gener-ous audiences than meetings planned for whites. In Philadel-phia, one meeting specifically for a black audience raised $60 to $70, while meetings for white audiences had raised only $40 and $50. One organizer observed, "The colored people of [Philadelphia] will do more for the [Africans] than the whites." Black churches also became involved in returning the men to Africa. J.W.C. Pennington, a black pastor in Hartford, organized a society dedicated to sending a black missionary back with the group.

Samuel D. Hastings to Lewis Tappan, May 27, 1841, Lewis Tappan Papers, Library of Congress, reel #6.

had by this time learned to speak and read English, read the news out loud to the group. Some abolitionist friends arrived soon after and confirmed the report. Finally, the captives could celebrate. "Me glad—me thank American men—me glad,"[49] Cinqué said.

Toward Home

Though they were free, the Africans could not go home immedi-ately. The Supreme Court had not ordered the president to send the men back to Africa, which meant that the former captives would have to raise the money for their passage. The *Amistad* Committee, which had helped them throughout their ordeal, asked for donations in newspaper advertisements. Churches, aid societies, and ordinary citizens contributed.

The *Amistad* Committee also arranged a speaking tour for the Africans. A small group of the men visited churches in New York, Philadelphia, and Boston. At each stop, crowds paid to hear the men read from the Bible, spell English words, and sing songs in Mende and English. The committee hoped that the men would continue speaking and studying Christianity in the United States for several years. Then, when they returned to Africa, they could become missionaries, converting other Africans to Christianity.

The Africans themselves were restless. They wanted to go home. In August, five months after the Supreme Court pronounced them free, one of the Africans, named Foone, drowned in a canal near where the group was staying. Some people believed that Foone had committed suicide, thinking he would never return home. It became clear to the abolitionists that the Africans should leave as soon as possible. On November 27, 1841, the Africans set sail for Africa from New York harbor. They later sent a note back to some abolitionist friends saying they had arrived safely. Most were never heard from again.

Notes

Introduction:
Slaveholders' Worst Nightmare

1. Quoted in Herbert Aptheker, *American Negro Slave Revolts*, 5th ed. New York: International Publishers, 1983, p. 307.

Chapter One: Slavery and Slave Rebellions in America

2. *Illustrated London News*, "Slave Auctions in Richmond, Virginia," February 16, 1861, pp. 138–40. http://cti.library.emory.edu/iln/browse.php?id=iln38.1075.038.

3. Alfred Farrell, "Sarah Ross," in *Born into Slavery: Slave Narratives from the Federal Writers' Project, 1936–1938.* Washington, DC: Library of Congress, Manuscript Division. http://memory.loc.gov/ammem/snhtml/snhome.htm.

4. Aptheker, *American Negro Slave Revolts*, p. 141.

5. Thomas Jefferson to James Monroe, November 18, 1800. *The Thomas Jefferson Papers.* http://memory.loc.gov/ammem/collections/jefferson_papers/

6. Thomas R. Gray, "The Confessions of Nat Turner," in *The Confessions of Nat Turner and Related Documents*, ed. Kenneth S. Greenberg. Boston: Bedford/St. Martin's, 1996, p. 40.

Chapter Two:
The Stono Rebellion

7. Quoted in Mark M. Smith, *Stono: Documenting and Interpreting a Southern Slave Revolt.* Columbia: University of South Carolina Press, 2005, p. 15.

8. Quoted in Smith, *Stono*, p. 15.

9. Quoted in Peter H. Wood, *Black Majority: Negroes in Colonial South Carolina from 1670 through the Stono Rebellion.* New York: W.W. Norton, 1974; reissued 1996, p. 318.

10. Quoted in Wood, *Black Majority*, p. 319.

11. Quoted in Smith, *Stono*, p. 18.

12. Quoted in Wood, *Black Majority*, p. 319.

13. Quoted in Wood, *Black Majority*, p. 308.

14. Quoted in Smith, *Stono*, p. 25.

15. Quoted in Wood, *Black Majority*, p. 323.

Chapter 3: Gabriel's Rebellion

16. Quoted in Aptheker, *American Negro Slave Revolts*, p. 226.

17. Quoted in Douglas R. Egerton, *Gabriel's Rebellion.* Chapel Hill: University of North Carolina Press, 1993, p. 51.

18. Quoted in Egerton, *Gabriel's Rebellion*, p. 69.

19. Quoted in Aptheker, *American Negro Slave Revolts*, pp. 223–24.

20. Quoted in Egerton, *Gabriel's Rebellion*, p. 106.

21. Quoted in Egerton, *Gabriel's Rebellion*, p. 111.

22. Quoted in Egerton, *Gabriel's Rebellion*, p. 77.

Chapter 4:
Denmark Vesey's Rebellion

23. Lionel H. Kennedy and Thomas

Parker, *The Trial Record of Denmark Vesey*. Boston: Beacon, 1970, p. 18.

24. Quoted in Kennedy and Parker, *Trial Record of Denmark Vesey*, pp. 33–34.

25. Quoted in David Robertson, *Denmark Vesey: The Buried History of America's Largest Slave Rebellion and the Man Who Led It*. New York: Alfred A. Knopf, 1999, p. 83.

26. Quoted in Douglas R. Egerton, *He Shall Go Out Free: The Lives of Denmark Vesey*. Madison, WI: Madison House, 1999, p. 183.

27. Quoted in Kennedy and Parker, *Trial Record of Denmark Vesey*, pp. 135–36.

28. Quoted in Egerton, *He Shall Go Out Free*, p. 190.

29. Quoted in Douglas R. Egerton, *Gabriel's Rebellion*. Chapel Hill: University of North Carolina Press, 1993, p. 227.

Chapter 5:
Nat Turner's Rebellion

30. Gray, "Confessions of Nat Turner," p. 46.

31. Quoted in Gray, "The Confessions of Nat Turner," p. 48.

32. Quoted in Gray, "The Confessions of Nat Turner," p. 51.

33. Quoted in Gray, "The Confessions of Nat Turner," p. 52.

34. Quoted in Gray, "The Confessions of Nat Turner," p. 52.

35. Quoted in Gray, "The Confessions of Nat Turner," p. 53.

36. Quoted in Stephen B. Oates, *The Fires of Jubilee: Nat Turner's Rebellion*. New York: Perennial, 2004, p. 117.

37. Quoted in Gray, "The Confessions of Nat Turner," p. 56.

38. Quoted in Gray, "The Confessions of Nat Turner," p. 57.

39. Quoted in Eric Foner, ed., *Great Lives Observed: Nat Turner*. Englewood Cliffs, NJ: Prentice Hall, 1971, p. 36.

40. Quoted in Aptheker, *American Negro Slave Revolts*, pp. 306–07.

41. Quoted in Aptheker, *American Negro Slave Revolts*, p. 307.

42. Quoted in Foner, *Great Lives Observed*, p. 8.

Chapter 6:
The *Amistad* Rebellion

43. Quoted in John Warner Barber, *A History of the* Amistad *Captives*. New Haven, CT: E.L. and J.W. Barber, 1840, p. 5. http://amistad.mysticseaport.org/library/.

44. Quoted in Mary Cable, *Black Odyssey: The Case of the Slave Ship* Amistad. New York: Viking, 1971, p. 75.

45. John Quincy Adams, *The Memoirs of John Quincy Adams*, ed. Charles Francis Adams, vol. 10. Philadelphia: J.B. Lippincott.

46. John Quincy Adams to Rodger Baldwin, March 9, 1841. John Quincy Adams Papers. www.masshist.org/adams_editorial.

47. Roger Baldwin to John Quincy Adams, March 12, 1841. John Quincy Adams Papers.

48. *Colored American*, "Postscript," March 13, 1841.

49. *Colored American*, "From the American Anti-Slavery Reporter," March 27, 1841.

For More Information

Books

Terry Bisson, *Nat Turner*. New York: Chelsea House, 2004. This book, part of the Black Americans of Achievement series, gives a detailed account of the Turner conspiracy. It has been reprinted several times.

Lillie J. Edwards, *Denmark Vesey*. New York: Chelsea House, 1990. This book, part of the Black Americans of Achievement series, describes the Vesey plot.

Walter Dean Myers, Amistad: *A Long Road to Freedom*. New York: Dutton, 1998. The author provides nuanced accounts of the *Amistad* proceedings and good information about the experiences of the Africans in New Haven.

Mark M. Smith, *Stono: Documenting and Interpreting a Southern Slave Revolt*. Columbia: University of South Carolina Press, 2005. This is the first collection to pull together the relevant historical documents on the Stono Rebellion as well as scholarly debates surrounding the incident.

Karen Zeinert, *The* Amistad *Slave Revolt and American Abolition*. North Haven, CT: Linnet, 1997. This book begins with Cinqué's capture in Africa and takes readers through the Middle Passage, rebellion, and events surrounding the trials.

Web Sites

Exploring *Amistad* at Mystic Seaport (http://amistad.mysticseaport.org). This excellent Web site has profiles of key players in the *Amistad* trial, clips from newspapers at the time, and a detailed time line of the trial. It also has copies of many original documents relating to the *Amistad* case.

***Amistad* America** (http://amistadamerica. org). This Web site for the Freedom Schooner *Amistad* provides information on the ports the replica of the *Amistad* ship will be visiting and provides an overview of the *Amistad* story.

Connecticut Freedom Trail (www.ctfree domtrail.com). This is the Web site for the Connecticut Freedom Trail, which highlights locations important to the history of Connecticut's black community, including those relevant to the *Amistad* case.

Documenting the American South (http://docsouth.unc.edu/index.html). This large and helpful Web site contains collections of primary resources on various southern topics including slave narratives and the role of the church in the southern black community. The Web site is sponsored by the University of South Carolina.

Death or Liberty—Gabriel, Nat Turner, and John Brown (www.lva.lib.va.us/ whoweare/exhibits/DeathLiberty/index

.htm). The Library of Virginia has created a Web site with information on rebellions that happened in its state: the Gabriel conspiracy, Nat Turner's rebellion, and the raid on Harper's Ferry by white abolitionist John Brown. The site includes original, scanned documents pertaining to the rebellions as well as easy-to-read text copies of the documents' contents.

The Massachusetts Historical Society (http://masshist.org/welcome).The Massachusetts Historical Society is the repository for all the papers of the Adams family, including those of John Quincy Adams, who defended the *Amistad* captives. Some documents written by John Quincy Adams are available online.

Born in Slavery: Slave Narratives from the Federal Writer's Project 1936–1938 (http://memory.loc.gov/ammem/snhtml/snhome.html). This Web site is maintained by the Library of Congress. It is an online collection of slave remembrances and photographs collected by the Works Progress Administration.

Museum Exhibits

Amistad—A True Story of Freedom. In this excellent, interactive exhibit at the Connecticut Historical Society in Hartford visitors can read about many of the important people involved in the *Amistad* trial, see documents relat-

ed to the trial, and even hear a re-creation of the debate over the *Amistad* case in the Supreme Court.

Cinqué Lives Here: *Amistad.* Artifacts from the collections of the New Haven Colony Historical Society. This small but interesting exhibit at the New Haven Colony Historical Society contains some one-of-a-kind *Amistad* artifacts: keys to the New Haven jail where the Africans were imprisoned, the sign from outside defense attorney Roger Baldwin's office, and the famous portrait of Cinqué painted by Nathaniel Jocelyn.

Videos

All We Want Is Make Us Free. This video on the *Amistad* story is accompanied by a thirty-four-page teacher's guide. Many public libraries own copies. The video was produced by the *Amistad* Committee, New Haven, CT and is available from Linnet Books, 2 Linsley Street, North Haven, CT.

Amistad. This feature-length film directed by Steven Spielberg was released in 1997. It stars Morgan Freeman, Anthony Hopkins, Djimon Hounsou, and Mathew McConaughey. Though the movie has been criticized for being historically inaccurate with respect to the trial, it does somewhat accurately re-create the world of the 1840s. Run time: 150 minutes.

Index

Picture Credits

Cover: © CORBIS
AFP/Getty Images, 82
© Bettmann/CORBIS, 24, 75, 89
© CORBIS, 17
Courtesy of Spring Park historic site, 40
Emanuel Ame, 53
Getty Images, 58
Hulton Archive/Getty Images, 13, 16, 21, 27, 28, 36, 39, 68, 85
North Wind Pictures, 5, 8, 10, 11, 23, 35, 46, 49, 63, 64, 71, 78
Private Collection, Peter Newark American Pictures/Bridgeman Art Library, 67, 83
The Art Archive/Culver Pictures, 50
© Underwood & Underwood/CORBIS, 80-81

About the Author

Jessica A. Gresko is a journalist and author with degrees in history and political science from Columbia University. At Columbia she wrote her thesis on the *Amistad* rebellion. A grant from the history department enabled her to do research with *Amistad* materials in New Haven, Hartford, and Farmington. Gresko's first book, on the 1960s, was published by KidHaven Press in 2004. She has written for *The Associated Press* and the *Los Angeles Times*.